THE RAPTURE:
WHEN DOES IT OCCUR?

An Explanation and
Biblical Evaluation
Of Four Answers

G. Michael Cocoris

©2007, 2025 by G. Michael Cocoris

All rights reserved. This publication may not be reproduced (in whole or in part, edited, or revised) in any way, form, or means, including, but not limited to electronic, mechanical, photocopying, recording or any kind of storage and retrieval system *for sale*, except for brief quotations in printed reviews, without the written permission of G. Michael Cocoris, 2016 Euclid #20, Santa Monica, CA 90405, michaelcocoris@gmail.com, or his appointed representatives. Permission is hereby granted, however, for the reproduction of the whole or parts of the whole without changing the content in any way for *free distribution*, provided all copies contain this copyright notice in its entirety. Permission is also granted to charge for the cost of copying.

Unless otherwise indicated, all Scripture quotations are taken from the New King James Version ®, Copyright © 1979, 1980, 1982 by Thomas Nelson, Inc. Used by permission. All rights reserved.

The interior and exterier by John T. Cocoris

TABLE OF CONTENTS

Chapter 1	Introduction	1
Chapter 2	Pre-tribulation Rapture	3
Chapter 3	Mid-tribulation Rapture	53
Chapter 4	Pre-Wrath Rapture	59
Chapter 5	Post-tribulation Rapture	71
Chapter 6	Conclusion	94
Bibliopraphy		95
About The Author		107

Chapter 1

INTRODUCTION

The word "rapture" does not appear in the Bible. It is from the Latin verb *rapere*, which means "to seize, to snatch, or to carry away." The Latin translation of 1 Thessalonians 4:17 used it to translate the Greek word "caught up."

Paul describes the Rapture, saying, "For the Lord Himself will descend from heaven with a shout, with the voice of an archangel, and with the trumpet of God. And the dead in Christ will rise first. Then we who are alive *and* remain shall be **caught up** together with them in the clouds to meet the Lord in the air. And thus, we shall always be with the Lord" (1 Thess. 4:16-17, bold type added). The Greek word translated "caught up" means "to seize, carry off by force, snatch out or away." Thus, while the English word "rapture" does not appear in the English translation of the Bible, the event is there.

The Greek word translated "caught up" in 1 Thessalonians 4:17 occurs 13 times in the New Testament. "It describes how the Spirit caught up Philip near Gaza and brought him to Caesarea (Acts 8:39). Paul uses it to describe his experience of being caught up to the third heaven, whether in or out of his body (2 Corinthians 12:2-4). Thus, there can be no doubt that it is describing an actual removal of people from the earth to heaven when it is used in 1

Thessalonians 4:17 of the rapture of the church" (Ryrie, *What You Need to Know About the Rapture*, p. 26, hereafter, *Rapture*).

The question concerning the Rapture is, "When will it take place?" Will it be before the Tribulation, sometime during it, or after it? In one sense, the answer is determined by the interpretation of a few passages of Scripture, such as 1 Thessalonians 5:9, which states, "For God did not appoint us to wrath, but to obtain salvation (deliverance) through our Lord Jesus Christ" and Revelation 3:10, where the Lord says, "I also will keep you from the hour of trial which shall come upon the whole world."

However, it is not quite that simple; the timing of the Rapture is a complex issue involving many factors. For example, when does the wrath of 1 Thessalonians 5:9 begin? What does the phrase "keep you from" in Revelation 3:10 mean? That is only the beginning. Other passages and topics are involved, including 1 Thessalonians 5:1-3, 2 Thessalonians 2:1-8, the explanation of the last trumpet, the Day of the Lord, cosmic disturbances, the resurrection, the judgments, "the end," etc.

There are four primary views on when the Rapture will occur. The following is a brief examination of each position. All of the pertinent passages and topics concerning the Rapture will be addressed under at least one of the four possibilities.

This material is from a chapter in *Biblical Prophecy*, which explains all aspects of prophecy in the Bible. It is available at *www.insightsfromtheword.com* under Theological Studies.

CHAPTER 2

PRE-TRIBULATION RAPTURE

The origin of the modern Pre-tribulation Rapture view can be traced to John Darby and the Plymouth Brethren in the early 1800s. Advocates of the Pre-tribulation Rapture include R. A. Torrey, A. C. Gaebelein, James M. Gray, Harry Ironside, Lewis Sperry Chafer, Charles Feinberg, John Walvoord, Charles Ryrie, Dwight Pentecost, and many others. The question is, "What is the biblical support for a Pre-tribulation Rapture"?

Deliverance from Wrath

The Time of the Rapture The Bible's most detailed description of the Rapture is in 1 Thessalonians 4:13-18. Immediately after the discussion of the Rapture in chapter 4, Paul discusses the *time* issue. He says, "But concerning the times and the seasons, brethren, you have no need that I should write to you" (1 Thess. 5:1). The Greek phrase "but concerning" (often translated as "now concerning") is used elsewhere by Paul to denote "a new and contrasting subject" (Ryrie, "The Church and the Tribulation: A Review," p. 175, who cites 1 Cor. 7:1, 7:25; 8:1; 12:1; 16:1, 16:12; 1 Thess. 4:9). The new and contracting subject is the times (the general period) and the seasons (a fixed period) of the Rapture. In other words, this passage is about the time of the Rapture.

Paul explains ("for"), "For you yourselves know perfectly that the Day of the Lord so comes as a thief in the night. For when they say, 'Peace and safety!' then sudden destruction comes upon them, as labor pains upon a pregnant woman. And they shall not escape. But you, brethren, are not in darkness so that that day should overtake you as a thief" (1 Thess. 5:1-4).

In other words, the believers in the church at Thessalonica knew the times and seasons of the Rapture because they knew the Day of the Lord comes as a thief in the night, that is, unexpectedly (1 Thess. 5:2), when people say, "peace and safety," sudden destruction will come upon them as labor pains upon a pregnant woman (1 Thess. 5:3). Note carefully that the time of the Rapture is related to the Day of the Lord, which will come unexpectedly: 1) when people say, "**peace and safety**," 2) with **sudden destruction**, 3) **as labor pains** upon a pregnant woman. Milligan, a Greek scholar (with Moulton. he co-authored the famous *Vocabulary of the Greek New Testament*.), says the Greek construction of 1 Thessalonians 5:3 indicates that "it is 'at the very moment when they are saying'" peace and safety that sudden destruction comes upon them (Milligan, p. 65).

Deliverance from Wrath Later in the passage, Paul adds, "God did not appoint us to wrath, but to obtain salvation (Greek: "deliverance") through our Lord Jesus Christ (1 Thess. 5:9). The Day of the Lord not only brings sudden destruction (1 Thess.

5:3), it brings wrath (1 Thess. 5:9). Isaiah says, "The day of the Lord comes, cruel, with both wrath and fierce anger, to lay the land desolate; and He will destroy its sinners from it." (Isa. 13:9). Believers ("we") will be delivered from the Day of the Lord (1 Thess. 5:1-3), a day of the Lord's wrath (1 Thess. 5:9; Isa. 13:9).

Thus, 1 Thessalonians 5:1-9 teaches:

1. The time of the Rapture is related to the Day of the Lord.
2. The Day of the Lord is a day of God's wrath.
3. Believers will be delivered (raptured) from the day of the Lord's wrath.

Since believers are delivered from the Day of the Lord (1 Thess. 5:2), the day of wrath (1 Thess. 5:9), the question is, "When does the day of the Lord's wrath begin?" Remember, according to 1 Thessalonians 5:1-3, the day of the Lord's wrath comes unexpectedly: 1) when people say, "**peace and safety**," 2) with **sudden destruction**, 3) as **labor pains** upon a pregnant woman. So, the question is, when will people say "peace and safety," and sudden destruction come, like a pregnant woman having labor pains? The answer is in Matthew 24.

When the disciples asked Jesus about the end times, Jesus said, "You will hear of wars and rumors of wars. See that you are not troubled, for all *these things* must come to pass, but the end is not yet. For nation will rise against nation and kingdom against kingdom. And there will be famines, pestilences, and earthquakes in various places. All these *are* the beginning of sorrows. Then, they will deliver you up to tribulation and kill you, and you will be hated by all nations for My name's sake. And then many will be offended, will betray one another, and will hate one another. Then, many false prophets will rise up and deceive many. And because lawlessness will abound, the love of many will grow cold. But he who endures to the end shall be saved. And this gospel of the kingdom will be preached in all the world as a witness to all the nations, and then the end will come. Therefore, when you see the 'Abomination of Desolation,' spoken of by Daniel the prophet, standing in the holy place (whoever reads, let him understand)" (Mt. 24:6-15).

Jesus describes a period with a beginning (Mt. 24:6, 8) and an end (Mt. 24:14). He identifies it by pointing to Daniel 9:27 (Mt. 24:15), where Daniel discusses God's program for Israel. All views of the Rapture agree that Daniel 9 indicates the 70th week is seven years before the Second Coming of Christ. It is commonly called the Tribulation.

Paul speaks about the Day of the Lord, and Jesus discusses the 70th week of Daniel (the Tribulation). Both mention several characteristics that are the same. For example, Paul mentions **birth pangs** (1 Thess. 5:3), and so does Jesus. The Greek word translated "sorrows" (Mt. 24:8) means "birth pangs," and it is the same Greek word that is used for birth pangs in 1 Thessalonians 5:3. Paul mentions **sudden destruction** (1 Thess. 5:3) and Jesus refers to war, famines, pestilence, and earthquakes, which result in sudden destruction. Paul speaks of **"Peace and safety."** That must describe a time before the 70th week of Daniel (the Tribulation) because it starts with war (Mt. 24:6-8) and gets worse from there to the point that the last half of the 70th week of Daniel (the Tribulation) will be "*great* tribulation, such as has not been since the beginning of the world until this time, no, nor ever shall be" (Mt. 24:21, italics added). The proof that "peace and safety" are before the 70th week of Daniel (the Tribulation) is at the beginning, "peace" is taken *"from the earth"* (Rev. 6:4, italics added; see the chart below that proves Mt. 24 and Rev. 6 are talking about the same period, the 70th week of Daniel, the Tribulation).

Ryrie says, "Even a superficial knowledge of the Tribulation does not give the impression that there will be any time of peace and safety except perhaps the very beginning—certainly not at the end" (Ryrie, *Rapture*, p. 91). Later, he adds that a lull during the Tribulation "is not even hinted at in the text. Even if one could imagine a lull in the military conflict during the concluding months of the Tribulation, how could it be said that people will experience safety when so many physical upheavals will be reshaping the earth? The last judgment of each of the series in Revelation reveals killing of martyrs (6:9), a meteor shower (6:13), earthquakes (6:14), torment like the sting of a scorpion (9:10), one-third of the population killed (9:18), people growling with their tongues because of pain (16:10), armies convening on, Armageddon (16:14) and widespread destruction (16:20-21)" (Ryrie, *Rapture*, p. 97).

Hodges says, "Some strange exegesis has resulted from the failure to recognize that 1 Thessalonians 5 speaks in terms of a familiar eschatological scene. For example, some have attempted to place the events of chapter 5 immediately before Christ's manifestation in glory at the end of the Tribulation. To do this, some post-tribulational expositors have postulated a brief period of tranquility just after the major judgments of the Tribulation have run their course and just before Christ appears. However, New Testament prophecy knows nothing of such an interlude. According to the Lord Jesus Himself, the Tribulation is so severe that it threatens man's extinction (Matthew 24:22). Furthermore, at the end of the Tribulation, the world's armies mobilize for the final battle of Armageddon (Revelation 16:13–16 and 19:19). Therefore, this kind of exposition does not deserve serious consideration" (Hodges, p. 27, fn., 14).

Lyle E. Cooper, author of *The Pre-Wrath Rapture Theory Exposed as False*, put it like this: "How anyone could imagine 'peace and safety' in the middle of great tribulation escapes me" (Cooper, p. 87).

Conclusion: The Day of the Lord in 1 Thessalonians 5 is the same as the 70th week of Daniel (the Tribulation) in Matthew 24. Therefore, since believers are delivered from the Day of the Lord (1 Thess. 5:2), which comes when people are saying **peace and safety**, and **sudden destruction** comes like **birth-pangs** (1 Thess. 5:3), and those things happen before and at the beginning of the 70th week of Daniel, the Tribulation (Mt. 24:6-8), believers are delivered from the 70th week of Daniel. In other words, since believers are delivered from the day of the Lord's wrath (1 Thess. 5), that is, the 70th week of Daniel (Mt. 24), commonly called the Tribulation, the time of the Rapture is before the Tribulation.

In addition, note the correlation between Matthew 24:4-8 and the first four seals of Revelation 6.

Matthew	Revelation
False Christ (24:4-5)	Antichrist revealed (6:2)
War (24:6)	War released (6:3-4)
Famines (24:7a)	Famine results (6:5-6)
Pestilence & Earthquakes (24:7b-8)	Death reigns (6:7-8)

Matthew 24:4-8 and Revelation 6:2-8 describe the same period. Therefore, since the first four seals of Revelation 6 are identical to the 70th week of Daniel, the Tribulation, in Matthew 24, which correlates with the day of the Lord's wrath in 1 Thessalonians 5 and believers are delivered from the day of the Lord's wrath, they are delivered from the first four seals of Revelation 6. In other words, the first four seals of Revelation 6 describe the wrath of God.

There are other indications that the first four seals in Revelation 6 describe the wrath of God.

The seals originate with God the Father. The introduction to the seals in Revelation 6 begins with God sitting on the throne (Rev. 4:2). "The 'throne' of Revelation 4:2, like the throne of Revelation 20:11, speaks of judgment; God as judge sits upon the throne" (McClain, p. 469). Therefore, the *seals are judgments that come from the throne of God.*

The seals are released by the Lion. In Revelation 5:2, a strong angel asked, "Who is worthy to open the scroll and loose its seal?" The answer is, "The Lion of the tribe of Judah, the root of David, has prevailed to open the scroll and to loose its seven seals" (Rev. 5:5). The title "Lion" refers to "Christ in His role as judge, rather than His role as Redeemer" (Van Kampen, *The Sign*, p. 182;). Van Kampen, the originator of the Pre-wrath Rapture position, also says, "Only the Lion of Judah (Christ as judge, not the Savior) can open the scroll, because God 'has appointed a day in which He will judge the world in righteousness through a Man whom He has appointed, having furnished proof to all men by raising Him from the dead (Acts 17:31)" (Van Kampen, *The Sign*, p. 319). "The judgment referred to here [Acts 17:31] will take place when Christ returns to earth to put down His enemies and begin His Millennial Reign" (MacDonald). He is the one who is "worthy to take the scroll, and to open its seals (Rev. 5:9, 12). He opens all seven seals (Rev. 6:1, 3, 5, 7, 9, 12, 8:1). *Baker's New Testament* says, "The Lamb opens all the seven seals of the scroll, and it is the Lamb who unleashes his fury against his opponents." The *wrath* of the Lamb is said to be involved (Rev. 6:16-17)."

The seals indicate that God is involved in what is happening. For example, a crown was "given" to the rider on the white horse (Rev. 6:2). The Greek word translated "crown" is the one used for the victor's crown (stephanos). Who gave the rider on the white horse the victory? The rider on the red horse was "granted ... to take peace from the earth, and that people should kill one another; and there was given to him a great sword" (Rev. 6:4). The rider did not do these things himself; they were "granted" and "given" to him. Who did the granting and giving? Rider on the pale horse was "given" the "power" to kill with the sword a fourth of the people on the earth (Rev. 6:8). Who gives the power to kill? James says, "There is one Lawgiver who is able to save and destroy" (Jas. 4:12). These riders were agents "appointed by God for a specific purpose" (Thomas, cited by Showers, p. 66).

The seals reveal instruments of God's wrath. The first seal is the coming of the Antichrist (Rev. 6:1-2). God has used Satan as an instrument of His wrath. "Again, the *anger* of the LORD was aroused against Israel, and He moved David against them to say, 'Go, number Israel and Judah'" (2 Sam. 24:1, italics added). "Now Satan stood up against Israel, and moved David to number Israel" (1 Chron. 21:1).

The second seal is war (Rev. 6:3-4). God has used war as an instrument of His wrath. In describing the war that the Lord will send against Babylon (Jer. 50:9), Jeremiah says, "Because of the wrath of the LORD, she [Babylon] shall not be inhabited, but she shall be wholly desolate. Everyone who goes by Babylon shall be horrified and hiss at all her plagues" (Jer. 50:13). Showers says, "The Scriptures clearly indicate that the wars of nations are often the weapons of God's wrath. For example, God declared that 'an assembly of great nations' would be 'the weapon of His indignation' and 'wrath,' even His Day of the Lord's wrath against Babylon (Isa. 13:1-5, 9, 17-19; Jer. 50:9, 13, 25). God raised up Syria and Phoenicia as instruments of His anger against Israel (Isa. 9:11-12). He used Assyria as 'the rod' of His anger, indignation, and wrath against Israel (Isa. 10:5-6). And He brought the Babylonians to war against Judah and Jerusalem as an expression of His wrath (2 Chron. 36:16-17; Ezra 5:12; Jer. 32:28-32)" (Showers, p. 65). "Gerhard Von Rad wrote, 'The prophets expected the day of Jahweh to bring war in its train'" (Von Rad, *Old Testament Theology*, 2:123, cited by Showers, p. 155).

The third seal is famine, which causes inflation (Rev. 6:5-6). God has used famine as an instrument of His wrath. "Take heed to yourselves, lest your hearts be deceived, and you turn aside and serve other gods and worship them, lest the Lord's anger be aroused against you and He shut up the heavens so that there be no rain, and the land yield no produce, and you perish quickly from the good land which the Lord is giving you" (Deut. 11:16-17).

Revelation 6:6 says, "I heard a voice in the midst of the four living creatures." Showers says, "The voice in the midst of the beast must belong to either God or Christ. Therefore, either God or Christ, not mankind or Satan, will administer the famine associated with the third seal" (Showers, p. 67).

The fourth seal is death (Rev. 6:3-4). Famine, death, and pestilence are spoken of in the Old Testament as God's wrath and the Day of the Lord. In Ezekiel 7, God repeatedly refers to His judgment as His anger (see "I will send My anger against you in verse 3, "Now upon you I will soon pour out My fury, and spend My anger upon you" in verse 8, and "My wrath *is* on all their multitude" in verse 14) and explains this judgment includes the sword, pestilence, and famine" (verse 15). Then, this is called "the day of the wrath of the LORD" (verse 19). In Revelation 1, Jesus said, "I have the keys of Hades and of death" (Rev. 1:18).

In the New Testament, God uses human government as an instrument of His wrath. Romans 13:4 says, "For it is a minister of God to you for good. But if you do what is evil, be afraid; for it does not bear the sword for nothing; for it is a minister of God, an avenger who brings wrath on the one who practices evil."

Paul Feinberg says, "To identify the wrath of God simply with His *direct* intervention is to overlook the fact that primary and secondary agency *both* belong to God. Would anyone *deny* that the Northern Kingdom had been judged by God because Assyria conquered her? Did the Southern Kingdom escape the wrath of God for her sin because the instrument of judgment was Nebuchadnezzar and Babylon? Surely, the answer is no. Then why should anyone think that because the early seals and trumpets relate to famine and war as well as natural phenomena, they cannot and are not expressions of the wrath of God?" (*The Rapture* by Archer, Feinberg, Moo, and Reiter, see pp. 61-63, italics his).

Van Kampen, the originator of the Pre-wrath view, acknowledges that "God often uses natural disaster and human means as instruments of judgment—as when He used 'Assyria [as] the rod of [His] anger' (Isa. 10:5)" (Van Kampen, *The Sign*, p. 322). In a footnote, he adds, "Many other Old Testament passages that depict God's wrath being expressed through war, famine, wild animals, or plagues are also marshaled to support this view (e.g., Lev. 26:21-28; Num. 11:33; 16:46; 25:8-11; Deut. 11:17; 32:22-25; 2 Chron. 29:8-9; 36:16, 17; Isa. 19:12; Jer. 14:12; 15:1-

9; 16:4, 10, 11; 19:7-9, 15; 21:5-7; 24:10; 48:8, 11-13; Ezek. 4:16, 17; 5:11-17; 6:3, 11, 12; 7:3, 8, 14, 19; 18:8; 21:19; 33:19-22; 38:19-22; 39:4)" (Van Kampen, p. 479, fn. 3). Commenting on the "noises, thunderings, lightnings, and an earthquake" in Revelation 8:5, Pre-Wrath advocate Kurschner remarks, "These are standard elements of judgment" (Kurschner, p. 89). Interesting. Pre-Wrath proponents recognize that such things as mentioned in the first seals are often used as means of God's judgment and wrath. They are even "standard elements" of God's judgment.

The seals reveal God's wrath. The sixth seal says the wrath of God "has come" (Rev. 6:17). Does that mean that the wrath of God comes before the sixth seal, at the point of the sixth seal, or, as some say, after the sixth seal? In the Greek text, the word "come" is in the aorist tense. The meaning of that in this passage is greatly debated. Rosenthal contends that it indicates the future. He says the expression "has come" in Revelation 6:17 means" is about to occur" (Rosenthal, p. 245). While the aorist can indicate the future, that is not its normal meaning. There must be compelling evidence for that to be the case.

The *context* of Revelation 6:17 indicates that "has come" is past, not future. The word "come" ties the first four seal judgments with the wrath in verse 17, which means the wrath in Revelation 6:17 goes back to the first seal. When each of the first four seals is open, one of the living creatures says, "Come and see" (6:1, 3, 5, 7). Then, in *response* to the four seal judgments, martyrs ask how much longer it will be before God judges those who dwell on the earth (Rev. 6:9-11). In *response* to the first four seals, the unsaved say the great Day of God's wrath has come. In other words, the structure of the chapter indicates that there are four seal judgments followed by the *response* of martyrs and then the *response* of unbelievers. In response to the four seal judgments, the unbelievers say God's wrath has come.

The *grammar* of "has come" indicates the past, not the future. Revelation 6:17 says, "The great day of his wrath has come." The Greek word translated "has come" is aorist indicative. What is the significance of an aorist indicative?"

Greek grammarians Dana and Mantey explain, "The important element of tense in Greek is *kind of action*. This is its fundamental significance. 'The chief function of a Greek tense is thus not to denote time, but progress' (Br. 6). For this element of tense, recent grammarians have adopted the German term *aktionsart,* 'kind of action.' The character of an action may be defined from either of three points of view: it may be continuous, it may be complete, or it may be regarded simply as occurring without reference to the question of progress. There are, therefore, three fundamental tenses in Greek: the present, representing continuous action; the perfect, representing completed action; and the aorist, ... representing indefinite action. 'These three tenses were first developed irrespective of time' (R. 824)... [Aorist] has time relations only in the indicative, where it is past and hence augmented. It has no distinctive form for present and future time, though the present and future tenses may denote an aoristic force. Modern Greek has developed a separate form for the aoristic future (T. 125).... There are really two fundamental ways of viewing action. It may be contemplated in a single perspective, as a point, which we may call *punctiliar* action (R. 823), or it may be regarded as in progress, as a line, and this we may call *linear* action (M. 109). The perfect tense is a combination of these two ideas: it looks in perspective at the action, and regards the results of the action as continuing to exist; that is, in progress at a given point. Hence, the perfect has both elements, linear and punctiliar. The aorist may be represented by a dot (•), the present by a line (-), and the perfect by the combination of the two (• -).... It is seen that the aorist has a 'punctiliar' action; that it regards the action as a point" (Dana and Mantey, pp. 178-179). Later, they say, "It has no essential temporal significance, *its time relations being found only in the indicative, where it is used as past and hence augmented*, (Dana and Mantey, p. 193, italics added). "Has come" in Revelation 6:17 is an aorist indicative, meaning, according to Dana and Mantey, it is a past event. Alfred's Greek New Testament says, "the virtually *perfect* sense of the aor. ἦλθεν here can hardly be questioned."

Ryrie points out that the Pre-wrath Rapture view says that the verb tense in Revelation 6:17 may mean "it is about to come," but "this is not how John uses it in other places in Revelation. In 11:18; 14:7, 15; 18:10, and 19:7, the same verb in the same tense as in 6:17 is used of events and people that are present and already on the scene, not that are about to come in the (howsoever near) future" (Ryrie, *Rapture*, pp. 94-95). All of Ryrie's examples are aorist indicative.

Pre-tribulation Rapture

1. The church will be delivered from the Day of the Lord (1 Thess. 5).
2. The Day of the Lord starts at the beginning of the Tribulation (Mt. 24; Rev. 6).
3. Therefore, the Rapture of the church is before the Tribulation.

Conclusion: Since the church is delivered from the Day of the Lord and the Day of the Lord starts at the beginning of the Tribulation, the Rapture takes place before the Tribulation, not in the middle of the Tribulation, sometime between the middle and the end of the Tribulation, nor at the end of the Tribulation. This is a case of summary judgment. Case closed. There is, however, more evidence, much more.

The Removal of the Restrainer

Do not Be Troubled "Now, brethren, concerning the coming of our Lord Jesus Christ and our gathering together to Him, we ask you, not to be soon shaken in mind or troubled, either by spirit or by word or by letter, as if from us, as though the day of Christ had come" (2 Thess. 2:1-2). In the Greek text, there is one article uniting "the coming of our Lord Jesus Christ" and "our gathering together to Him." "This is a definite allusion to the rapture he described in 1 Thessalonians 4:13-18" (Barnhouse, p. 96).

There is a textual problem with the phrase "the day of Christ." The critical text reads, "the day of the Lord." If the Day of the Lord is the correct reading, the believers at Thessalonica thought the Tribulation had come. The majority of manuscripts, however, contain the phrase "the day of Christ."

What is the meaning of "the Day of Christ?" Some students of the Scripture contend that the Day of Christ is another term, at least in this passage, for the Day of the Lord (Mason Jr., p. 359). Others contend that where "the Day of Christ" and similar expressions, such as "the Day of our Lord Jesus Christ," "the Day of Jesus Christ," and "the Day of the Lord Jesus," appear elsewhere in the New Testament, they refer to the Judgment Seat of Christ (1 Cor. 1:8; 5:5; 2 Cor. 1:14; Phil. 1:6, 1:10; 2:16).

Thus, the believers at Thessalonica were disturbed because they thought they had received some communication indicating they had missed the Rapture ("the coming of our Lord Jesus Christ and our gathering together to Him") and the Judgment Seat of Christ ("the day of Christ").

Do Not Be Deceived Paul adds, "Let no one deceive you by any means for *that Day will not come* unless the falling away comes first" (2 Thess. 2:3a, NKJV including italics). He told them not to be *shaken in mind* or *troubled* (2 Thess. 2:2). Now he adds that they should not be *deceived*.

The italicized words in 2 Thessalonians 2:3 indicate that the words "that day will not come" are not in the Greek text. Also, the Greek word translated "comes" is an aorist, which describes a completed act. A better translation is "has come." In other words, Paul is simply saying that they should not be *deceived* because, first, the falling away has to occur, meaning that it has not happened yet. At this point, he is describing what must happen first in what is commonly called the Tribulation.

The Greek word translated "falling away" means "defection, apostasy, revolt." Outside the Bible, it was used for political defection; however, in the Greek translation of the Old Testament, called the Septuagint, and in the New Testament, it always refers to a religious revolt (Milligan; see Acts 21:21, the only other instance of this word appearing in the New Testament). This Greek word "denotes a deliberate abandonment of a formally professed position or view, a defection, a rejection of her former allegiance" (Hiebert, p. 305). This verse is not talking about a general apostasy. In the Greek text, the article "the" occurs before "falling away." Verse 5 indicates that the Thessalonians knew which apostasy Paul spoke about; we do not.

Paul adds, "and the man of sin is revealed, the son of perdition, who opposes and exalts himself above all that is called God or that is worshiped, so that he sits as God in the temple of God, showing himself that he is God" (2 Thess. 2:3b-4). They should not be *deceived* because the man of sin has to be revealed and that hasn't happened yet either.

The man of sin is commonly called the Antichrist. "He will be revealed, at least to discerning people, when he makes a covenant with many of the Jewish people (Dan. 9:27)" (Ryrie, commentary on Thessalonians, p. 104). That will signal the start of the Tribulation. Paul reminds them, "Do you not remember that when I was still with you, I told you these things?" (2 Thess. 2:5). Brainard says that Paul's argument is "the antichrist is proof that the day of the Lord is here" (Brainard, p. 55). "If you see the antichrist, you are in the day of the Lord. If you don't see the antichrist, then you are not in the day of the Lord" (Brainard, p. 56).

Restrainer Removed The third thing Paul says is, "And now you know **what** is restraining, that he may be revealed in his own time. For the mystery of lawlessness is already at work; only who now restrains will do so until **He** is taken out of the way. And then the lawless one will be revealed" (2 Thess. 2:6-8a, bold type added). *The restrainer must be removed before the lawless one is revealed.* Verse 6 says, "What is restraining" (in Greek, "what" is neuter) and verse 7 says, "he who now restrains ... until he is taken out of the way" (in Greek, "he" is a masculine pronoun). So, the restrainer is both a power and a person. What or who is the restrainer?

Answers range from the apostle Paul to Satan. One of the most common is that the Restrainer is the Roman government and the Roman emperor. Those who hold to this view contend that the Roman Empire suppressed evil through its advanced system of laws. The problem with this position is that the Roman Empire collapsed, was removed, so to speak, and the Antichrist was not revealed. Some say the restrainer is Michael the archangel.

Another possibility is that the restrainer is the Holy Spirit. He fits the description of both neuter and masculine. In Greek, the word "spirit" is neuter, but the Holy Spirit is referred to by the masculine pronoun "He" (e.g., Jn. 14:17). Also, the Restrainer must restrain the Antichrist, who Satan energizes. Therefore, the Restrainer must be more powerful than Satan himself. Not even Michael the archangel was that powerful (Jude 9). Only God qualifies, and He is here as the person of the Holy Spirit. By the way, even though Pre-Wrather Van Kampen thinks the restrainer in this passage is Michael, he says, "At the appearance of Christ coming (*parousia*), Antichrist will again feel the effects of restraint, but this time the one who restrains will be Christ, not Michael" (Van Kampen, *The Sign*, p. 328). Interesting. God restrains the Antichrist.

How can it be said that the Holy Spirit will be removed? People will be saved during the Tribulation, which can only happen if the Holy Spirit is present. The answer is that the Holy Spirit was "here" in the Old Testament, and people were saved. Yet Jesus said the Holy Spirit would "come" at Pentecost (Jn. 16:13). The Holy Spirit "came" at Pentecost to baptize believers into the body of Christ (Acts 1:5; 11:15-16; 1 Cor. 12:13). He will be removed, then, in the sense that He will no longer be baptizing people into the body of Christ, yet He will still be here in the sense of doing His regenerating work. If what is being removed is the Holy Spirit in His baptismal work, when the Holy Spirit is removed, the body of Christ, the church (Eph. 1:22-23), goes with Him.

To sum up, Paul tells believers at Thessalonica not to be disturbed by being deceived because the Restrainer has not been removed. "Since the removal of the Restrainer takes place before the manifestation of the lawless one, this identification implies a pretribulational rapture" (Hiebert, p. 313).

By the way, reading this passage in Greek convinced J. N. Darby of the Pre-tribulation Rapture (Brainard, p. 54).

Conclusion: Since the church is delivered from the Day of the Lord and the Day of the Lord is synonymous with the Tribulation, the church is raptured before the Tribulation.

Kept from the Hour

In the letter to the church in Philadelphia, Jesus said, "Because you have kept My command to persevere, I also will keep you from the hour of trial which shall come upon the whole world, to test those who dwell on the earth" (Rev. 3:10). This verse speaks of a trial that will "come upon the whole world." As commentators point out, this is the Tribulation, "the "troublous times, which precede the Parousia" (Swete), "the tribulations, which are prophesied later in the book" (Hatch, cited by Smith), "the period of testing and tribulation that precedes the establishment of the eternal kingdom" (Mounce). Ryrie says, "that this promise concerns the church's relation to the Tribulation period is almost never debated (posttrib Douglas Moo acknowledges this as well). The reason is in the verse itself. This time of trial "is about to come on all the inhabitants of the earth." It is worldwide and on the inhabited earth—that is, on its people" (Ryrie, *Rapture*, p. 112).

Correct Translation The way Revelation 3:10 is translated, it seems as if Jesus is saying that because they have kept His command to persevere, He will keep them from the Tribulation. Is perseverance the requirement to be kept from the Tribulation? No. "Because you have kept my command to persevere" should be connected with the last part of verse 9. The correct translation reads: "Indeed, I will make them come and worship before your feet, and to know that I have loved you because you have kept My command to persevere." The phrase "because you have kept My command to persevere" only goes with "I will make them come." In other words, Jesus says, "I will make them come" (Rev. 3:9) and ... I will *also* keep you from the hour of trial" (Rev. 3:10, italics added). The presence of the word "also" supports this explanation of the passage (for a detailed explanation and defense of this translation, see Niemelä, pp. 14-39).

Kept from the Hour The promise is that believers will be kept *from* the hour of trial. Some say that "from" should be translated "through" (Swete, who thinks they will be kept, that is, preserved "in any trial;" Mounce), but "through" or "in" is most assuredly *not* the normal way to translate "from" (ἐκ) and there are Greek words that mean "through" (δια) and "in" (εν). Pollock points out that of the over 890 times the Greek word ἐκ is used in the New Testament, only once is it translated "thought," and in that verse, Galatians 3:8, it means "by" (A. J. Pollock, *Will the Church Go Through the Great Tribulation?* p. 11, cited by Stanton, p. 49). Moreover, it is simply not true that Tribulation saints going "through" the Tribulation will be preserved. Many of them will be killed (Rev. 6:9-11; 7:7,14; 13:7).

According to Arndt and Gingrich, the recognized authority on the meaning of Greek words, the Greek word "from" (ἐκ) means "from, out of, away from." Its first meaning is used "to denote separation from." [For example, John 20:1 says, "The stone had been taken away (αἴρω) from (ἐκ) the tomb." The stone was removed from outside the tomb; it did not emerge from within the tomb.] More specifically, under that meaning is listed a subcategory, "situations and circumstances out of which someone is brought," and Revelation 3:10 is listed there and it is said to mean to "keep from" (Arndt and Gingrich, p. 234).

Furthermore, the combination "keep from" is only used in one other place in the New Testament, and, as in Revelation 3, it is spoken by Jesus and recorded by John. Jesus says, "I do not pray that You should take them out of the world, but that You should keep them from the evil one" (Jn. 17:15). He is praying for "complete exemption" (Ryrie, *A Survey of Bible Doctrine*, p. 170). He is praying that believers will not fall into the clutches of Satan at all, not that they be seized and then delivered (Stanton, fn., p. 49).

This complete deliverance is not through the trial or in the trial. It is not even from the trial. It is from the *hour* of the trial, that is, the period of time (Walvoord; Smith). "Note the words KEEP FROM. This phrase does not mean *keep from harm* while in the hour, or *persevere* while in the hour, or *protect* while in the hour. It means *kept from the hour,* which implies removal prior to the hour" (Brainard, p. 47).

Ryrie illustrates the point by saying that if he, as a teacher, told the class that all A students would be exempt from the exam, they would not know whether or not they should come to class on the day of the test. He could mean that he would give them the exam and also provide them with a sheet containing the answers. On the other hand, if he said that all A students would be excused from the hour of the test, they would know that they did not have to come to class. They would be exempt from the time of the exam (Ryrie, *Basic Theology*, pp. 484-485).

Since Revelation 3:10 says the church will be delivered from the Tribulation that occurs just before the Second Coming, it teaches that the Rapture will take place before the Tribulation. This does not apply to just one local church. All seven letters in Revelation 2-3 end by saying, "Hear what the Spirit says to the churches," which is also added to the end of this letter (Rev. 3:13).

Conclusion: Revelation 3:10 indicates a Pre-tribulation Rapture.

The Church is Not on Earth During the Tribulation

In Revelation, the word "church" (singular) appears seven times and the word "churches" (plural) occurs twelve times. Eighteen of the nineteen are in chapters 1-3. The nineteeth occurrence is in Revelation 22. Neither the word "church" nor the word "churches" appears in Revelation 6-18, the chapters describing the Tribulation. If the church is in the Tribulation, why is it not mentioned by name *during* the Tribulation in Revelation 6-18?

This is not an argument *from* silence; it is an argument *about* silence! In his letters to churches, Paul included a prayer. The fact that there is no prayer at the beginning of Galatians is an indication that he was not thankful for them because they had so soon departed from the gospel. It would be like a girl always addressing her boyfriend in her letters with the greeting "My dearest John" and then writing a letter that said, "Dear John." The absence of "My dearest" would immediately send the signal to John that something was different.

In Revelation 2-3, the expression "To him who has an ear, let him hear what the Spirit says to the churches" occurs seven times (Rev. 2:7, 11, 17, 29; 3:6, 13, 22). A similar expression occurs in Revelation 13:9, which says, "If anyone has an ear, let him hear." Why is the expression "what the Spirit says to the churches" omitted in Revelation 13:9, even though it appears seven times in Revelation 2-3? In Revelation 13:9, the Spirit is speaking to "anyone," not the churches, because the churches are not present during that time.

Revelation 22:16 says, "I, Jesus, have sent My angel to testify to you these things in the churches. I am the Root and the Offspring of David, the Bright and Morning Star." The book of Revelation was written *to* the churches; not all of it is *about* the church. The subject of the book of Obadiah is "judgment on Edom." Almost the entire book is about Edom, but the book is written to Israel.

Ryrie puts it like this, "The word *church* occurs 18 times in chapters 1, 2, and 3, and once in chapter 22. The phrase "wife of the Lamb" appears once in chapter 21. Yet in chapters 4-18, there is silence about the church, which indicates to pretribulationists that the church will not be present on the earth during the Tribulation years" (Ryrie, *Rapture*, p. 55).

I asked Arnold Fruchtenbaum what he thought was the greatest argument for the Pre-tribulation Rapture. His reply was the absence of the word "church" in Revelation 4-18.

Conclusion: The church is not on the earth during the Tribulation.

The Church is In Heaven During the Tribulation

Revelation 4 says, "And behold, a throne set in heaven and One sat on the throne. And He who sat there was like a jasper and a sardius stone in appearance; and there was a rainbow around the throne, in appearance like an emerald. Around the throne were twenty-four thrones, and on the thrones, I saw twenty-four elders sitting, clothed in white robes, and they had crowns of gold on their heads. And from the throne proceeded lightnings, thunderings, and voices. Seven lamps of fire were burning before the throne, which are the seven Spirits of God" (Rev. 4:2b-5).

The Throne The occupant of the throne is not identified in these verses, but later, John says the One who "sat on the throne (Rev. 4:2) is the "Lord God Almighty" (Rev. 4:8), that is, God the Father.

The Elders Around the throne of God are twenty-four thrones occupied by twenty-four elders, clothed in white robes and wearing gold crowns. The identity of the twenty-four elders has been a subject of extensive debate. Who are the *twenty-four* elders?

The twenty-four elders are clothed in white (Rev. 4:4). The church at Sardis was told that *overcomers* would be "clothed in white garments" (Rev. 3:5), and the church at Laodicea was counseled to buy "white garments" (Rev. 3:18), and now the elders in heaven are clothed in white robes (the Greek word translated "robes" in Rev. 4:4 is the same one rendered "garments" in Rev. 3:5, 18).

The twenty-four elders wear crowns of gold (Rev. 4:4). Members of the church are told they will receive crowns (Rev. 2:10; 3:11). Crowns were only promised to the church (Smith). "They are already rewarded. That means they have already participated in the resurrection. In Revelation, except for Christ, the twenty-four elders are the only ones who wear gold crowns (Smith). There are two Greek words for crowns, one for a sovereign (diadem) and the other for a victor (stephanos). The latter one is used in Revelation 2:10, 3:11, and here. In this case, however, the ones wearing the crown sit on thrones.

The twenty-four elders are redeemed, resurrected, and rewarded. Therefore, the twenty-four elders are overcomers from the church who will rule on the earth (Rev. 5:10). They cannot be angels because the blood of the Lamb does not redeem angels. They cannot be Old Testament saints or tribulation martyrs because "those two classes don't receive the rewards until they are raised at the second coming" (Brainard, p. 61).

That does not mean that only 24 will rule. The twenty-four elders represent the overcomers as the elders represented the church at the Jerusalem Council in Acts 15 (Smith). "It is evident, too, that the elders are a representative group. Twenty-four would come far short of being a sufficient number to come out of every kindred and tongue and people and nation" (Smith, p. 116).

Some suggest the number twenty-four is probably an allusion to 1 Chronicles 24, where there were twenty-four courses of priests (Smith). As the twenty-four orders of priests represented the thousands of priests, the twenty-four elders here represented the overcomers from the church. Brainard, however, says, "As there were 24 courses of priests in the temple service in the Old Testament, so there must be 24 courses of priests in the New Testament priesthood. This is not the New Testament copying the pattern seen in the Old Testament. It is actually the other way around. The arrangement in order of the temple in the Old Testament was patterned after the arrangement and order of the true temple in heaven (Heb. 8:5)" (Brainard, p. 63).

The combination of white robes, gold crowns, and throne-sitting is enough to prove that the twenty-four elders represent overcomers from the church, but there is more. In chapter 5, John says, "Now when He had taken the scroll, the four living creatures and the twenty-four elders fell down before the Lamb, each having a harp, and golden bowls full of incense, which are the prayers of the saints. And they sang a new song, saying: 'You are worthy to take the scroll, and to open its seals; for You were slain, and have redeemed **us** to God by Your blood out of every tribe and tongue and people and nation, and have made **us** kings and priests to our God; and we shall reign on the earth'" (Rev. 5:9-10, bold type added).

In the Greek text, the living creatures are neuter, the elders are masculine, and "each" is masculine. Therefore, what follows "each" in verse 8 through 10 is a reference to the elders (Smith). The elders have a harp and a bowl of incense, which is symbolic of the prayers of the saints (Ps. 141:2). "They" sing a new song, saying Jesus is worthy to open the scroll because He was slain, redeemed "us," and made "us" to reign on the earth. Who are the "they," who sing a new song? The English translation sounds as if both the four living creatures and the elder sing. The Greek text, however, indicates that only the elders sing at this point.

There is a textual problem with "redeemed *us*" in Revelation 5:9. The TR, MT, and Sinaiticus (א) contain the word "us" (ἡμᾶς), but the Critical Text omits the word "us." According to the apparatus in the Critical Text, the word "us" is in *every manuscript* except Alexandrinus (A)! There are 24 manuscripts of Revelation 5. The word "us" is in 23 of them. The textual evidence is overwhelming in favor of "us."

In his *Greek New Testament According to the Family 35*, Pickering asked, "Why do you suppose that the NU [Critical Text] follows a single MS of demonstrably inferior quality in Revelation (objectively so) against virtually all others (perhaps six scattered curses have 'our' for 'us') plus lat., syr., bo.? And why do the editors of modern versions follow their lead?" (Pickering, p. 522). There is simply no doubt that the correct reading of Revelation 5:9 is "us," which means that the twenty-four elders are singing about their redemption. The fact that the twenty-four elders sing about their redemption eliminates the possibility that the twenty-four elders are angels; angels are not redeemed.

There is also a textual problem with "made *us* kings and priests" … and *we* shall reign on the earth" in verse 10. The TR reads "us" and "we," but the MT and the Critical Text read "made *them*" … "And *they* will reign." (Thus, the NASB supplies "men" in verse 9 and translates verse 10 "made them" and "they will reign;" NIV supplies "persons" in verse 9 and translates verse 10 "made them" ... "and they will reign;" ESV supplies "people" in verse 9 and translates verse 10 "made them" ... "and they shall reign"). The fact that in Revelation 1:5, John says that Jesus "has made us kings and priests" supports the reading of "us" and "we" in Revelation 5:10.

The reading of the critical text of Revelation 5:10 ("us" and "we") would not change the identity of the twenty-four elders. McClain says, "As Hengstemberg pointed out long ago, the elders speak of *themselves with* the redeemed in verse 9, whereas in verse 10, they speak objectively of the church *as its representatives*, which they are in chapters 4 and 5" (McClain, italics in his quotation). John Niemela, who takes the critical reading of verse 10, suggests there is an antiphony in verses 9 and 10 so that the twenty-four elders are singing in verse 9 and they are being responded to in verse 10 (see the article at https://www.pre-trib. org/articles/dr-john-niemela/message/revelation-5-the-twenty-four-elders-and-the-rapture/watch).

McClain says, "It is an impressive fact that, in the long and bewildering history of attempts to interpret the symbols of the Apocalypse, there is hardly any instant of greater unanimity than with reference to that of the twenty-four elders. Among the well-known commentators who regard these elders as representatives of the church are Alford, Barnes, Benson, Binney, Carpenter, Clarke, Clemance, Brook, Crafer, Crosby, Dusterdieck, Fausset, Giedlestone, Godet, Gray, Henry, Holden, Kuyper, Milligan, Plummer, Robertson, Scott, Sheppard, Simcox, Smith, Swete,

Weider. [To that list could be added Walvoord, Pentecost, Ryrie, etc.] Vincent says, 'The twenty-four elders are usually taken to represent the one Church of Christ.' And Hengstemberg declares, 'That the elders are representative of the church, there can be no question.' The commentators named represent many eschatological viewpoints. They are not writing in support of any pretribulation school of thought. As a matter of fact, they are in sharp disagreement with one another about much in the book of Revelation.... Yet in spite of the disagreements, they are united in the opinion that the twenty-four elders of chapters 4 and 5, enthroned in heaven, do represent the true Church of God!" (McClain, p. 471).

Ryrie puts it like this, "Most identify the 24 elders as representing the church, and since they are seen in heaven in Revelation 4:4 and 5:8-10, the church is mentioned as in heaven. Some think this argument is no good because the critical text of 5:9-10 has the elders singing about redemption in the third person, as if redemption were not their own experience (thus, they could not represent the church, which has been redeemed). But this is a weak argument; after all, Moses sang of redemption in the third person right after he experienced it (Exodus 15:13, 16-17)" (Ryrie, Rapture, p. 56).

The picture presented of the twenty-four elders indicates that they are redeemed, resurrected, and rewarded (they have "crowns" and are on "thrones;" see Walvoord, p. 118). The fact that they had been rewarded indicates that the Judgment Seat of Christ has already taken place, which means that the Rapture has already taken place. In addition, their place in Revelation (chapters 4 and 5) indicates they were raptured *before the Tribulation,* which starts in chapter 6.

Conclusion: The church is in heaven during the Tribulation.

Normal Activities, Peace, and Safety

The "Olivet Discourse" is a two-chapter (Mt. 24-25) explanation of prophecy delivered by Jesus. Along with Daniel and Revelation, the Olivet Discourse is one of the Bible's most important passages on prophecy. It has been said, "No passages are more important" (Cooper, p. 4).

The Questions As Jesus and the disciples left the Temple, the disciples commented on the magnificence of the Temple buildings. Jesus responded by saying that the Temple would be destroyed. Then, they walked from the Temple through the Kidron Valley to the Mount of Olives. Once on the Mount of Olives, which overlooked the Temple, "The disciples came to Him privately, saying, "Tell us, when will these things be? And what *will be* the sign of Your coming and of the end of the age?" (Mt. 24:3). The disciples asked two questions, one about the time and the other about the sign. Jesus answers the question about the sign first and then about the time.

The Sign Jesus describes a period that has a beginning (Mt. 24:8) and an end (Mt. 24:14). This period will be characterized by 1) false Christ (Mt. 24:4-5), 2) war (Mt. 24:6-7a), 3) famines (Mt. 24:7b), 4) pestilences (Mt. 24:7c), 5) earthquakes (Mt. 24:7d), 6) persecution (Mt. 24:9-13), and 7) the worldwide preaching of the gospel (Mt. 24:14).

Then Jesus concludes ("therefore" in verse 15) that during the period He just described, the Abomination of Desolation spoken of by Daniel the prophet will occur. The period is the 70th week of Daniel (Dan. 7:27), which is seven years in length and commonly referred to as the Tribulation. The Abomination of Desolation occurs in the middle of those seven years. Notice this is a *flashback*. The period ends in verse 14 and verse 15 is a flashback to the middle of the 70th week of Daniel.

For those living when the Abomination of Desolation takes place, Jesus gives two commands. The first is to flee without taking anything with them (Mt. 24:16-22). The second command is not to be deceived by messianic claims (Mt. 24:23-28).

Jesus adds, "Immediately after the Tribulation of those days, the sun will be darkened, and the moon will not give its light; the stars will fall from heaven and the powers of the heavens will be shaken. Then the sign of the Son of Man will appear in heaven, and then all the tribes of the earth will mourn, and they will see the Son of Man coming on the clouds of heaven with power and great glory. And He will send His angels with a great sound of a trumpet, and they will gather together His elect from the four winds, from one end of heaven to the other" (Mt. 24:29-31).

To sum up, the Abomination of Desolation will occur in the middle of the Tribulation. That will begin the Great Tribulation, immediately after which the Lord will return to the earth. The sign of the coming of Christ will be the Abomination of Desolation.

Pre-tribulation Rapture

Jesus pointed that out when He said, "Therefore, where you *see* the abomination of desolation in Matthew 24:15 and "When you *see* all these things, know that it is near—at the doors!" in Matthew 24:33-34 (italics added). The sign of the end will be "the sign of the Son of Man will appear in heaven" in Matthew 24:30.

The Time. At this point in the passage, Jesus addresses the time issue (Mt. 24:32). Alexander remarks, "Having answered the question as to the *signs* of His return in judgment, He now answers that as to time."

First, Jesus talks about what *can* be known. "Now learn this parable from the fig tree: When its branch has already become tender and puts forth leaves, you know that summer *is* near. So, you also, when you see all these things, know that it is near; at the doors!" Assuredly, I say to you, this generation will by no means pass away till all these things take place. Heaven and earth will pass away, but My words will by no means pass away" (Mt. 24:32-35).

Because fig trees produce new leaves late in the spring, the presence of leaves indicates summer is near. Likewise, those living at the time when these things begin to occur should be able to read the signs of the times. The generation that is alive when these events occur will not pass away until all these things happen. Heaven and earth will be replaced with a new heaven and a new earth, but the word of Jesus Christ is eternal. Jesus' word can be totally trusted.

Second, Jesus talks about what *cannot* be known. "But of that day and hour no one knows, not even the angels of heaven, but My Father only" (Mt. 24:36). In the Greek text, verse 36 begins with a construction that should be translated "now concerning" (περι δε), instead of "but." It introduces a new subject (Mt. 22:31; Mk. 12:26; 13:32; Acts 21:25; 1 Cor 7:1; 8:1; 12:1; 16:1,12; 1 Thess. 4:9, 13; 5:1). At this point, it is obvious that the Lord is abruptly saying something different. He just said there are signs that people at the time *can and should know* (Mt. 24:33). Now, He says *no one knows* the "day and hour." The issue of "not knowing" is repeatedly emphasized in Matthew 24:36-44 (see Mt. 24:36; 24:39; 24:42; 24:43; 24:44) and beyond (Mt. 24:50; 25:13). In addition, the change from the plural "those days" in verse 29 to the singular "that day" in verse 36 also implies a change of subject.

The question is, "The day and hour of what?" There are two answers. One answer is that the day and the hour refer to the Second Coming. The arguments for that explanation are: 1) The passage's context is about the Second Coming at the end of the Tribulation (Mt. 24:37). 2) The illustration of the flood indicates that the people were taken in judgment (Mt. 24:38-39; so Walvoord; Pentecost; Toussaint).

The other answer is that the hour and the day refer to the Rapture, which will be before the Tribulation. This is another *flashback* (see the comments on 24:15 above). Several indications say this is the correct interpretation. For example, the context indicates that this is *not* a reference to the end of the Tribulation. The end of the Tribulation is so bad that unless those days were shortened, no one would be saved (Mt. 24:22). Yet Matthew 24:38 indicates that what is being talked about here is the activities of ordinary life (France).

"But as the days of Noah *were,* so also will the coming of the Son of Man be. For as in the days before the flood, they were eating and drinking, marrying and giving in marriage, until the day that Noah entered the ark and did not know until the flood came and **took** them all away, so also will the coming of the Son of Man be. Then, two *men* will be in the field: one will be **taken** and the other left. Two women will *be* grinding at the mill: one will be **taken** and the other left" (Mt. 24:37-41, bold type added).

In the days of Noah, people did not know when the flood was to come. Likewise, people will not know when the coming of the Son of Man will be. The Lord explains ("for") how the days *before* the flood are like the days preceding the coming of the Son of Man; people were carrying on with life as usual. They are eating, drinking, and getting married! This is a description of family life. Men working in the field signifies nothing more than the normal course of life. Women grinding at a mill is as ordinary as men working in a field. Tasker points out that cultivating the fields (Mt. 24:40), grinding corn at the mill (Mt. 24:41), enjoying fellowship, and marrying and giving in marriage are "usual occupations." In the days before the flood, people were preoccupied with their *ordinary activities,* unaware of the flood's beginning.

What is described here starkly contrasts what will happen at the end of the Tribulation (Mt. 24:21-22). Just before the Rapture, life will be relatively "normal." It is just before the Rapture that people will be saying peace and safety (1 Thess. 5:3). That is why, for them, the Lord will come as a thief in the night (Mt. 24:43; 1 Thess. 5:2; 2 Pet. 3:10). On the other hand, just before the Second Coming, things will be so bad that unless those days be shortened, no flesh will survive (Mt. 24:21-22).

Another indication that this is about the Rapture is that the Greek word translated "taken" in Matthew 24:40 and 41, concerning the flood, is different from the one translated "took" in verse 39, concerning men in the field and women at the mill. The one used in verses 40 and 41 means "to take to or with oneself" (A-S), "to take into close association, take (to oneself), take with/along" (BDAG; see also 1:20-21; 2:13, 14, 20, 21; 17:1). It is used of the Rapture in John 14:3. Lane says that the word for "took" (αιρω) in the previous verse [Mt. 24:39] suggests taking away with violence as with the flood, but Christ drops that word here and says that by His coming, one should be taken away with Him as a friend takes a companion (Lane, p. 313). France points out that it implies "to take someone to be with you, and, therefore, here points to salvation rather than the destruction of the one "taken." He says, "two different words appear for the action of taking."

Even Gundry, who takes this passage to refer to a Post-tribulation Rapture, argues that its details prove that it is the Rapture. He says, "Two different words appear for the action of taking, αιρω (vv. 39) and παραλαμβανω (vv. 40, 41). The same word could easily have been employed had an exact parallel between the two takings been intended. Instead, we have the employment of another word, which only two days later describes the Rapture (John 14:3). The example of the Deluge illustrates not so much the judgmental character of the Parousia as its unexpectedness so far as the wicked are concerned" (Gundry, p. 138).

Pre-tribulationists who say that Matthew 24:37-41 does not refer to the Rapture, use Luke 17:34-36, the parallel passage to Matthew 24:37-4,1, to support their position. That passage says, "'I tell you, in that night there will be two *men* in one bed: the one will be taken and the other will be left. Two *women* will be grinding together: one will be taken and the other left. Two *men* will be in the field: the one will be taken and the other left.' And they answered and said to Him, 'Where, Lord?' So, He said to them, 'Wherever the body is, there the eagles will be gathered together.'" Based on Luke 17:37, they conclude that the ones taken are taken to judgment and, therefore, Matthew 24:37-41 is talking about the Second Coming and judgment rather than the Rapture.

Luke 17:37 has been explained in several different ways. Geldenhuys, who believes Luke 17:37 is referring to unbelievers at the Second Coming of Christ, says, however, "In replying to the inquisitive question as to where the unredeemed will be left, the Savior gives no direct answer, but in what is probably a well-known Palestinian proverb points out that where there is spiritual decay, judgment will follow relentlessly and assuredly." Notice that he interprets the question to mean where the unbelievers are *left* for judgment, not taken to judgment.

The Rapture: When Does It Occur?

Hart, who believes Matthew 24:37-41 refers to the Rapture, says, "Without excluding a possible allusion to judgment, a better suggestion is that the disciples meant, 'Where are You to be revealed, Lord?' This understanding of Luke 17:37 fits the parallel passage in Matt 24:28, where the proverbial saying applies exclusively to the Parousia (24:29–31)." He interprets the question to mean where will the Lord be. Marshall agrees. He believes that Luke 17:37 refers back to v 23 ("Men will tell you, 'There He is!' or 'Here He is!'), not the immediately preceding context. Verse 37 acts as a climax for the whole sermon and appears to summarize the broad central theme of Christ's return. As such, the proverbial saying about the vultures expresses the truth that 'the world unmistakably will know … where the Son of Man returns.' While the idea of judgment may be included in the disciples' question of Luke 17:37, the verse and its context do not confirm unequivocally that the one who is taken is taken in judgment" (Hart, pp. 63-64).

So, what does Luke 17:34 mean? The issue is the meaning of the question, "Where, Lord?" Were they asking where the unbelievers would be taken to judgment, where the unbelievers would be left, or where the Lord would be? Verse 36 ends with "and the others left." So the proverb, "vultures gather where dead bodies are," is answering the question, "Where will the unbelievers be left," not where they will be taken. So, Luke 17:34=37 is not talking about the Second Coming and judgment; it is talking about the Rapture, as is Matthew 24:37-41.

Pre-tribulation Rapture

Interpreting Matthew 24:36-41 as the Rapture is not essential to the Pre-tribulation Rapture. In fact, most Pre-tribulationists do not believe that the Olivet Discourse is talking about the Rapture, including Charles C. Ryrie, E. Schuyler English, J. Dwight Pentecost, Renald Showers, Gerald B. Stanton, Stanley D. Toussaint, John F. Walvoord, etc. They interpret the ones taken as those taken to judgment. Among the few Pre-tribulationists who think Olivet Discourse speaks about the Rapture are J. F. Strombeck, Zane Hodges, Ray C. Stedman, Arnold G. Fruchtenbaum, Dave Hunt, etc.

Conclusion: The presence of normal activities, peace and safety before the Tribulation indicates the Rapture will be before the Tribulation.

Imminence

The word "imminence" means "pending." The concept is that something *may* happen shortly, or it *may* not. It is pending. In contrast, "soon" means "shortly, before long," it *must* happen. The New Testament does not teach the "soon" coming of Christ; it teaches the "imminent" coming of Christ. He *could* rapture believers any minute, but He may not. If the Rapture is imminent, it is before the Tribulation. Here are some verses that teach the "imminent" coming of Christ. Many of the commentators who claim these verses indicate imminency are not Pre-tribulationists.

1 Thessalonians 4:15 Paul thought he could be alive when the Lord came back. He says, "For this, *we* [Paul, Silvanus, and

Timothy; see 1 Thess. 1:1] say to you by the word of the Lord, that *we* who are alive and remain [he just used "we" to refer to himself, Silvanus, and Timothy] until the coming of the Lord will by no means precede those who are asleep. For the Lord Himself will descend from heaven with a shout, with the voice of an archangel, and with the trumpet of God. And the dead in Christ will rise first. Then, *we* who are alive and remain shall be caught up together with them in the clouds to meet the Lord in the air. And thus, we shall always be with the Lord" (1 Thess. 4:15-17, italics added). Paul personally expected the Rapture to occur in his lifetime. He uses the first personal pronoun, "we," to talk about those alive at Christ's coming (1 Thess. 4:15, 17). His use of the personal pronoun "we" implies, even demands, that Paul expected that he, Silvanus, and Timothy would personally be alive at the return of Christ.

Many commentators concur. Lightfoot says, "The apostles certainly do believe as though there was a reasonable expectation for the Lord's appearing in their own time. They used modes of expression that cannot otherwise be explained. Such is the use of the plural here." Alford states, "Then beyond question, he himself expected to be alive together with a majority of those to whom he was writing at the Lord's coming. Commenting on the use of the plural, Milligan says, "There can be no doubt that the passage naturally suggests that they expected so to survive…and we must not allow the fact that they were mistaken in this belief to deprive their words of their proper meaning." Frame states that by using the word "we," "Paul thus betrays the expectation that he and his contemporary Christians will still remain alive until Christ comes."

These four well-respected, scholarly commentators were not defending the Pre-tribulation Rapture; they were simply expounding the text. Paul expected to be alive because he believed in the imminent return of Christ for His saints. That does not mean that Christ *had* to come back during Paul's lifetime, but that He *could* come back at any moment, which means He could have come back during Paul's lifetime.

James 5:8 James says, "The coming of the Lord is at hand" (Jas. 5:8). The Greek adverb translated "at hand" means "near" (A-G). It is used for being nearby in space. For example, "He was near Jerusalem" (Lk. 19:11). It is used of being near in time. The "Feast of Tabernacles was at hand" (Jn. 7:2). Concerning James 5:8, Moo states, "The early Christians' conviction that the *parousia* was 'near' or 'imminent' meant that they fully believed that it *could* transpire within a very short period of time—not that it *had* to." It loses its punch if this verse is not teaching an any-moment Rapture. Believers could be bitter for a while, and when they see that they are in the Tribulation, they can repent before the Lord returns. Mitton says, "James clearly believed, as others of his time did, that the coming of Christ was imminent. Since then, there was not long to wait; his plea for patience is greatly reinforced."

Philippians 4:5 Paul says, "The Lord is at hand" (Phil. 4:5). This could mean the Lord is near in the sense that His presence is close or that His return is imminent. The latter possibility is the view taken by most commentators. James 5:8 proves that it is correct. It says, "The *coming* of the Lord is at hand."

Romans 13:12 Paul says, "The day is at hand." In this context, Paul is, at least, referring to the Rapture because he says, "Our salvation is nearer than when we first believed" (Rom. 13:11). Hodges says that "the day" is the Day of the Lord, which is the way that expression is used many times in the Old Testament. Cranfield, who does not believe in the Pre-tribulation Rapture, says, "The meaning here must be that the day is imminent. We might paraphrase verse 12a: 'The night is almost over, the day is almost come.' We have then, in the first half of the verse, an instant of the New Testament insistence on the nearness of the End.... It is well known that very many scholars regard it as assured results that the primitive Church was convinced that the End would certainly occur within, at the most, a few decades and that its conviction has been refuted by the indisputable fact of 1900 years of subsequent history." After the comments just quoted, he pens two pages to explain that the statement "the night is far spent, the day is at hand" means in the words of Calvin, "that from the time when Christ once appeared there is nothing left for the faithful except always to look forward to His second coming with minds alert."

Hebrews 10:25 The writer to the Hebrews says, "as you see the Day approaching." The Greek word translated "approaching" is the Greek word translated "at hand." It indicates imminence (Guthrie).

Pre-tribulation Rapture

First Peter 4:7 Peter declares, "The end of all things is at hand." Barnes notes, "The word rendered 'is at hand (ἤγγικε) may refer either to proximity of place or time, and it always denotes that the place or the time referred to was not far off.... The idea as applied to time, or to an approaching event, is undoubtedly that it is close by; it is not far off; it will soon occur."

Revelation 22:10 John says, "The time is at hand. (Rev. 22:10). The expression "at hand" eliminates the possibility of it meaning "expectation," because of the way it is used in these verses. You would not translate Romans 13:12 "the day is expecting," 1 Peter 4:7 the end of all things is expecting," or Revelation 22:10 the time is expecting."

James 5:9 James says, "The Lord is standing at the door" (Jas. 5:9). This vividly portrays the "nearness" of the judgment (Mitton; Alford). "To reinforce his warning, James reminds his readers again that this judgment is imminent" (Moo).

Hebrews 10:37 The writers to the Hebrews says, "For yet a little while, and He who is coming will come and will not Tarry" (Heb, 10:37). "The original has a very emphatic phrase (μικρὸν ὅσον ὅσον) to imply the nearness of Christ's return, "yet but a very, very little while.... Christians felt sure that Christ's coming was very near" (*The Cambridge Bible for Schools and Colleges*). This verse means, "Christ comes quickly and will not delay" (*Baker's New Testament*). "Soon the Redeemer will appear to deliver his afflicted people from all their sorrow; to remove them from a world of pain and tears; and to raise their bodies from the dust, and to receive them to mansions where trials are forever unknown" (*Barnes Notes*).

The Rapture: When Does It Occur?

Revelation 22:7 Jesus says, "Behold, I am coming quickly! Blessed is he who keeps the words of the prophecy of this book." The Greek word translated "quickly" is the adverb form of the word rendered "shortly" in the previous verse. The thought here is that Christ will come suddenly (Smith) or that Christ's coming is pending (Walvoord), that is, that His coming is imminent (Smith; Morris). "As John saw it, the coming of Christ would take place at any moment" (Barclay). This is a warning to be alert (Walvoord).

Revelation 22:12 Jesus also says, "And behold, I am coming quickly, and My reward is with Me, to give to everyone according to his work." Walvoord makes an interesting connection, "When the One who exists from eternity states, 'Behold, I come quickly,' it means that from the divine point of view, end-time events are impending." When He arrives, Christ will reward everyone based on their works. This refers to the Judgment Seat of Christ (2 Cor. 5:10-11; Walvoord).

Revelation 22:20 John says, "Even so, come, Lord Jesus!" John anticipates Jesus coming quickly. He invites Jesus to come—now! Does that not indicate imminence? If anything had to be fulfilled before Jesus could come, how could John end by inviting Jesus to come? To say the same thing another way, if something had to be fulfilled, John would have ended by saying something like, "Now you know to look for the Antichrist."

The New Testament speaks of believers eagerly waiting for the Lord (1 Cor. 1:7; Phil. 3:20-21; 1 Thess. 1:9-10; Titus 2:13). The opponents of imminency say these verses are talking about expectation, not imminency. Showers points out, "The term *imminent* is an adjective used to describe the nature of an event. It depicts the kind of event that is always hanging overhead and could happen at any moment. In contrast, the term *expectant* is an adjective used to describe people's attitude toward an event.... Thus, the expectant Rapture could be an imminent rapture" (Showers, p. 203, italics his). Believers in the New Testament were expecting the Lord to come, alright; they were expecting Him to come imminently!

In 2 Peter 3:4, Peter says, "Where is the promise of His coming? For since the fathers fell asleep, all things continue as they were from the beginning of creation." Scoffers were bringing up the fact that the Lord had not returned. That was a problem only because believers were expecting the Lord to come in their lifetime.

The opponents of imminency argue that imminence is incorrect because the New Testament states that certain events must occur before the Lord returns, such as the death of Peter. J. Barton Payne was a Post-tribulationists who denied the doctrine of imminency. Showers, who studied under him in graduate school, said Payne "denied a belief in imminency of Christ's coming only in 'the early apostolic church,' not in the latter part of the apostolic church" (Showers, p. 204).

Yet, after stating that denial, Payne wrote, "Even in those early days, the days could have come about during the lifetime of those addressed. Indeed. The attitude that it should so come about is expectantly taught by inspiration [Payne cites Paul's use of "we" in 1 Thess. 4:15, 17; 1 Cor. 15:51" (Payne, *The Imminent*

Appearing of Christ, p. 90, cited by Showers, p. 204).

In fact, Payne was convinced that 11 New Testament passages taught the imminent coming of Christ (Mt. 24:2-25:13; Lk. 12:36-40; Rom. 8:19, 23, 25; 1 Cor. 1:7; Phil. 3:20; 4:5; 1 Thess. 1:9-10; Titus 2:12-13; Jas. 5:7-8; Jude 21; Rev. 16:15)" (Payne, pp. 95-103, cited by Showers, p. 206). Concerning imminency, Payne even said, "In fact, no natural reading of the Scripture would produce any other conclusion" (ibid., p. 102, cited by Showers, p. 206).

Showers adds, "Dr. Payne asserted that in John 21:22-23, the apostle John indicated that the church in the latter part of the apostolic age believed that Christ would come before he (John) would die (ibid., p. 91)" (Showers, p. 204). By telling Peter, "If I will that he [John] remain until I come, what is that to you?" (Jn. 21:22), is not Jesus teaching the possibility that He could come back at any moment? John 21:23 says, "Then the saying went out among the brethren that this disciple would not die." In other words, the brethren believe that Jesus *would* come back before Peter died. John clarified by adding, "Yet, Jesus did not say to him that he would not die, but, 'If I will that you remain until I come" (Jn. 21:23), that is, Jesus did not mean that He *would* come back, but He *could* come back.

Even Van Kampen says, "Christians expected to witness Christ return in their lifetime. Perhaps their expectations for Christ's soon return came as a result of Christ's instructions to Peter on how he would die" [John 21:18–19] (Van Kampen, *The Sign*, p. 252).

Pre-tribulation Rapture

If the Rapture is imminent, nothing has to happen before the Rapture. Therefore, the Rapture is before the Tribulation. Walvoord says, "If the Scripture presents the coming of the Lord for His church as imminent by so much, they also declare it as occurring before the predicted period of the tribulation" (Walvoord, p. 82).

If the Pre-tribulation Rapture is not true, then instead of the Lord being at hand (Phil. 4:5), He is at least 3½ to 7 years away. Instead of looking for Christ coming from heaven (Phil. 3:20), we should be looking for the Antichrist signing a treaty on earth (Dan. 9:27). Instead of looking for the appearance of our great God (Titus 2:13), we should be looking for the Abomination of Desolation.

Conclusion: Imminency indicates a Pre-tribulation Rapture.

Many more arguments are used to support a Pre-tribulation Rapture. Walvoord lists fifty (John F. Walvoord, *The Rapture Question*, pp.191-199).

Summary: The evidence for the Pre-tribulation Rapture includes deliverance from wrath (the Tribulation), removal of the Restrainer, promise that the church will be kept from the *time* of the Tribulation, absence of the word "church" in Revelation 4-19, the identification of the elders in Revelation 4, the normal activities, peace, and safety before His coming, and imminency.

Although not listed in this chapter as one of the proofs of the Pre-tribulation Rapture, Dispensationalism is a factor in deciphering what the Scripture says about the Rapture. For example, the 70th week of Daniel is clearly for the Jewish people (see Dan. 9:24; 12:7; Mk.

13:9; Lk. 21:12). In the Olivet Discourse, when Jesus talked about the Tribulation, He referred to the Temple, Jerusalem, the Sabbath, and the elect as a reference to the Jewish people. In Revelation, not only is the church not mentioned in chapters 6-18, but Jewish references abound (the 144,000, the two witnesses, the nation of Israel, and Jerusalem). Brainard wrote that the saints in the Tribulation are "Jewish believers in the Messiah to serve God through the Mosaic law, with a particular focus on the temple service" (Brainard, p. 37).

In the Bible, types are illustrations. Enoch is translated to heaven (Gen. 5:24). Is that a type of the Rapture? Is the fact that he was translated before the flood in Genesis 6 a type of the Pre-tribulation Rapture? God once judged a whole city, Sodom. He rained fire and brimstone from heaven, as He will do again during the Tribulation. Before He poured out His judgment on Sodom, He pulled out His children. Likewise, before God pours out judgment again, this time on the whole world, He will pull out His bride, the church. John is "called up" to heaven (Rev. 4:1). Is that a type of the Rapture? Brainard points out, "This journey to heaven is a type of the pretribulation Rapture. It follows the church age in the second and third chapters, presents the church in the throne room of God in the fourth and fifth chapters, and precedes the start of the tribulation with the opening of the seals in the sixth chapter" (Brainard, p. 62).

Brainard also says, "We recognize a picture of the truth (for that is what a type is) only after we have become familiar with the truth. But once we are grounded in the truth, the types for that truth will present themselves in the pages of Scripture" (Brainard, p. 65). Keep in mind that types are not proof; they are illustrations.

In John 13, Jesus told the disciples that He was about to leave (Jn. 13:33) and He told Peter that he would deny Him three times (Jn. 13:38). It is unfortunate that there is a chapter break at this point because, in the original, the next statement is Jesus saying, "Let not your heart be troubled, you believe in God, believe also in me. In My Father's house are many mansions; if it were not so, I would have told you. I go to prepare a place for you. And if I go and prepare a place for you, I will come again and receive you to Myself; that where I am, there you may be also" (Jn. 14:1-3). They were no doubt disturbed by what Jesus told them, but Jesus told them not to be troubled because of what they knew about the future, namely that He was going to prepare a place for them and come back for them, take them to that place He had prepared for them. Likewise, we should be comforted. The Lord is coming back for His bride, the church and His coming is imminent. It is before the Tribulation.

CHAPTER 3

MID-TRIBULATION RAPTURE

Mid-tribulation Rapture is the view that the Rapture will occur in the middle of the seven-year Tribulation. Its "principal expositor" is Norman B. Harrison (Walvoord, p. 171), who presents the case for the Mid-tribulation Rapture in his book *The End: Rethinking the Revelation* (1941). Others holding this view include J. Oliver Buswell, Gleason Archer, and Harold J. Ockenga. It has not been widely embraced; only a small minority of expositors have held this position. Walvoord suggests this will be the case in the future (Walvoord, p. 189).

According to the Mid-tribulation view: 1) The Rapture takes place at the last trumpet (1 Cor. 15:52). 2) The last trumpet in Revelation is the seventh trumpet (Rev. 11:15). 3) The last trumpet is in the middle of the Tribulation, which is the beginning of the Great Tribulation and God's wrath (see Rosenthal, p. 57). Thus, the two decisive issues in the Mid-tribulation position are 1) the identification of the trumpet in 1 Corinthians 15:52 with the seventh trumpet in Revelation 11:15 and 2) the insistence that the seventh trumpet is in the middle of the Tribulation.

The Last Trumpet

The Last Trumpet In 1 Thessalonians 4, when Paul describes the Rapture, he speaks of "the trumpet of God" and the dead being raised (1 Thess. 4:16). In 1 Corinthians 15, he says, "Behold, I tell you a mystery: we shall not all sleep, but we shall be changed in a moment, in the twinkling of an eye, at the last trumpet. For the trumpet will sound, and the dead will be raised incorruptible, and we shall be changed" (1 Cor. 15:51-52). Thus, at the Rapture, "the trumpet of God" is sounded and it is called the last trumpet.

The word "last" can mean "last in a point of time" or "last in a sequence" (Harrison, p. 75; Pentecost, p. 189). Schoolchildren know that the bell for the end of the first class is not the last bell for the day. It will be followed by a first bell for the next hour (Walvoord, p. 185). The last trumpet of 1 Corinthians 15 is the last trumpet of the church, calling the church on earth to meet the Lord in the air. There are no more trumpets *for the church*, but there are other trumpets after that.

The Seventh Trumpet John writes, "Then the seventh angel sounded: and there were loud voices in heaven saying, 'the kingdoms of this world become the kingdoms of our Lord and His Christ and He shall reign forever and ever!'" (Rev. 11:15). At first, the identification of the seventh trumpet in Revelation with the last trumpet in 1 Corinthians 15:52 seems appropriate, but after only a little reflection, it is apparent that the two are not identical—at all.

Mid-tribulation Rapture

Paul wrote 1 Corinthians in AD 57. John wrote Revelation around AD 95. Paul was definitely not thinking about the seventh trumpet of Revelation when he penned 1 Corinthians 15:52. He could not have. Revelation had not been written yet. It would not be written for another 38 years! Perhaps it could be argued that the Holy Spirit had the connection in mind (Harrison, p. 75), and Paul was not aware of it, but in light of what else is known about the comparison, that is highly unlikely, if not impossible.

The seventh trumpet in Revelation 11:15 is the trumpet of an angel. The "last trumpet" of the Rapture in 1 Corinthians 15:52 is called the "trumpet of God." Furthermore, the seventh trumpet in Revelation is a symbol of judgment on the earth during the Tribulation. The last trumpet of 1 Corinthians 15 is a signal for the church to meet the Lord in the air,

The "most damaging fact" against Mid-tribulation Rapture, the one that "alone spells the doom of Mid-tribulationism" (Walvoord, pp. 184-185), is that the seventh trumpet in Revelation is not the last trumpet! After the coming of Christ, the elect will be gathered "with a great sound of a trumpet" (Mt. 24:31). So, there will be a "last trumpet" at the Rapture and a trumpet blast to gather the elect at the beginning of the kingdom.

Conclusion: The last trumpet for the Rapture is not the seventh trumpet of Revelation.

The Seventh Trumpet

Harrison says, "The Day of Wrath has only now come (Rev. 11:18). This means that nothing that proceeds in the Seals and Trumpets can rightfully be regarded as wrath" (Harrison, p. 119). In other words, he claims that the seven seals and the first six trumpets are related to the first half of the Tribulation and the seventh trumpet is in the middle of the Tribulation, which is the beginning of the Great Tribulation and the wrath of God. Walvoord says it is not too much to say that Mid-tribulation depends on the theory that the seventh trumpet of Revelation begins the Great Tribulation, which is in the middle of the Tribulation (Walvoord, pp. 172-173).

The problem with Harrison's view is that according to the sixth seal, "the great day of His wrath has come" (Rev. 6:17). He interprets the sixth seal "as reaching to the day of Wrath" (Harrison, p. 120). Pardon the pun, but that is indeed a stretch. The text says that it "*has* come," meaning that it came before the time of the sixth seal (see the discussion of Revelation 6:17 in the chapter on Pre-tribulation above).

In addition, Revelation 7:14 is the only specific reference to "the Great Tribulation" in the entire book of Revelation and it is between the seals and the trumpets, indicating that the Great Tribulation begins somewhere in the seal judgments. Pointing to Revelation 6:17 and Revelation 11:18, both of which say that God's wrath "has come," Pentecost concludes that "neither the seals nor the trumpets can be divorced from the divine program associated with the pouring out of wrath upon on the earth"

Mid-tribulation Rapture

(Pentecost, *Things to Come*, p. 184).

The fatal blow to Mid-tribulationism is that it places the seventh trumpet in the middle of the Tribulation. The seventh trumpet is clearly at the end of the Tribulation because when it is sounded, "the kingdoms of this world have become the kingdoms of our Lord and of His Christ" (Rev. 11:15). That happens at the end of the Tribulation, not in the middle of the Tribulation.

Conclusion: The seventh trumpet is not in the middle of the Tribulation.

Summary: Mid-tribulation Rapture (identifying the last trump in 1 Corinthians 15 and 1 Thessalonians 4 with the last trump in Revelation and designating the last trump in Revelation as taking place in the middle of the Tribulation) is not biblical.

CHAPTER 4

PRE-WRATH RAPTURE

In 1986, a Christian businessman named Bob Van Kampen began discussing the timing of the Rapture with Marvin Rosenthal, the Director of The Friends of Israel Gospel Ministry. Van Kampen had questions about the Pre-tribulation Rapture; Rosenthal had been committed to it for 35 years. For the next several years, they spent a great deal of time discussing the timing of the Rapture.

In 1990, Rosenthal wrote the book *The Pre-Wrath Rapture of the Church*. That launched the Pre-Wrath position. Rosenthal acknowledges that Bob Van Kampen planted the seed of the book in his mind. Rosenthal told Bob, "Without you, there would have been no book" (Rosenthal, p. xiv; for the complete story, see pp. 17-36). In 1992, Van Kampen, the originator and first advocate of the Pre-Wrath Rapture (Showers, p. 7), wrote *"The Sign,"* and in 1997, *"The Rapture Question Answered."* In 2001, Renald Showers, a long-time friend of Van Kampen and Rosenthal, wrote *The Pre-Wrath Rapture View, an Examination and Critique*. It is a definitive answer to the Pre-Wrath view.

The Name The name "Pre-Wrath" is unfortunate. Pre-tribulationism, Mid-tribulationism, and Gundry's Post-tribulationism teach that the church will not go through the wrath of God. Therefore, they are Pre-wrath! They differ on when the wrath of God begins. Is the wrath of God poured out at the beginning, in the middle, sometime during the second half, or at the end of the Tribulation?

Tom Ice has dubbed the Pre-Wrath Rapture position the Three-Quarter Tribulation Rapture. The advocates of that view would say that title is not accurate because all they are claiming is that the Rapture takes place "sometime" after the middle of the 70th week and before the end of the 70th week. Since Pre-Wrath Rapture is the name of the position, it will be used here.

An Explanation The 70th week of Daniel 9 consists of seven years, commonly referred to as the Tribulation. The Pre-Wrath view divides the 70th week into three parts (Rosenthal, p. 233): 1) The first half of the 70th week of Daniel 9, which lasts 3½ years. 2) The Great Tribulation (Mt. 24:21), which begins in the middle of the 70th week, will be cut short and, therefore, will not last 3½ years. 3) Cosmic disturbances appeared before the Day of the Lord, which begins after the Great Tribulation and lasts until the end of the 70th week

According to the Pre-Wrath interpretation of the 70th week, the order of events is as follows: 1) The first half of the 70th week consists of the beginning of birth pains (Mt. 24:4-8), which are the first four seals (Rev. 6:1-8). 2) The Great Tribulation (Mt. 24:21) begins in the middle of the 70th week with the breaking of the fifth seal (Rev. 6:9-11) and will be cut short with the cosmic disturbances of the sixth seal (Mt. 24:21-22; Rev. 6:12-14) sometime between the middle and the end of the 70th week. 3) The church will be raptured between the sixth and seventh seals (Rev. 7:9-14). 4) Cosmic disturbances come before the Day of the Lord, which begins with breaking the seventh seal (Rev. 8:2).

> Middle of 70th Week = Great Trib. (shorten)→Rapture →Day of the Lord (wrath)

The Pre-Wrath explanation contains many distinctive interpretations of Scripture, but the two most critical are: 1) The Great Tribulation will be shortened (Mt. 24:22). Rosenthal says, "The shortening of the Great Tribulation to less than 3½ years is one of the most important truths to be grasped if the chronology of the end times events is to be understood" (Rosenthal, p. 111). 2) Cosmic disturbances come before the Day of the Lord (Joel 2:30-31), which starts after the close of the Great Tribulation. Rosenthal says the Day of the Lord is the watershed issue (Rosenthal, pp. 140, 176). He concedes, "If the seventh week is the Tribulation period, or 'the time of wrath' and God's people are exempt from 'wrath,' the matter is settled" (Rosenthal, p. 106). In other words, if the entire Tribulation is the day of wrath, the Pre-tribulation Rapture is correct.

The Shortening of the Great Tribulation

Pre-Wrath View Jesus says, "There will be great tribulation, such as has not been since the beginning of the world until this time, no, nor ever shall be. And unless those days be shortened, no flesh will be saved; but for the elect's sake those days will be shortened" (Mt. 24:21-22). The Greek word translated "shortened" means "to cut off, amputate," hence, "to curtail, shortened" (A-S), "mutilate, curtail," figuratively, "shortened" (A-G).

The Pre-Wrath view correctly states that the 70th week of Daniel lasted for seven years and the Great Tribulation begins in the middle of the 70th week of Daniel. All other explanations of the 70th week of Daniel claim that the Great Tribulation will last for 3½ years. What is unique to the Pre-Wrath interpretation is that the Great Tribulation will be cut short to less than 3½ years. Rosenthal says the Great Tribulation "is less than three and one-half years in duration. It begins in the middle of the 70th week, but does not run until the end of the 70th week" (Rosenthal, p. 109). If that interpretation of the Great Tribulation is not correct, the Pre-Wrath interpretation collapses. When Jesus says the Great Tribulation will be shortened, did He mean shortened to 3½ years or shortened to less than 3½ years?

Daniel 12 When Jesus spoke about the Great Tribulation, which has never been, nor shall never be again, He alluded to a passage in Daniel. When Daniel was told, "There should be a time of trouble such as never was since there was a nation, even to that time" (Dan. 12:1), he asked, "How long shall the fulfillment of these wonders be?" (Dan. 12:6). He was told that it would be "for a time, times, and half a time" (Dan. 12:7). In other words, this period, which is like no other, called the Great Tribulation in Matthew 24:21, will last 3½ years, not less than 3½ years. Showers explains it this way: "Because the Great Tribulation will begin in the middle of the seventh week, this statement [Daniel 12:7] means that it will last throughout the entire second half of the seven-year seventh week" (Showers, p. 21, italics added). Therefore, by "shorten," Jesus means to 3½ years, not less than 3½ years. If Jesus is saying less than 3½ years, He is contradicting Daniel 12.

Revelation 12 In Revelation 12, the Devil is kicked out of heaven (Rev. 12:9), which takes place in the middle of the Tribulation. At that point, Satan knows that he has a short time (Rev. 12:12). Exactly how much time does he have? Israel flees into the wilderness where she is protected from Satan "for a time, times, and half the time (Rev. 12:14), that is 3½ years. Satan works through the beast, another name for the Antichrist, who is "given authority to continue for 42 months" (Rev. 13:5), that is 3½ years. Note carefully: in Revelation 12 and 13, a "short time" is defined as 3½ years, not less than 3½ years. The fact that Revelation 12 and 13 refer to the wrath of Satan, not the wrath of God, does not matter. The point is in the context of the second half of the Tribulation, a "short time" is defined as 3½ years, not less than 3½ years.

Conclusion: Contrary to the Pre-Wrath position, "shortened" is not less than 3½ years.

Cosmic Disturbances

Pre-Wrath View The concept is that the cosmic disturbances preceding the Day of the Lord is essential to the Pre-Wrath view.

That concept is based on verses in Joel 2, which says, "And I will show wonders in the heavens and in the earth: Blood and fire and pillars of smoke. The sun shall be turned into darkness, And the moon into blood, before the coming of the great and awesome Day of the LORD" (Joel 2:30-31, italics added; see also Mal. 4:5, which says Elijah will come before the "great and dreadful day of the Lord").

Joel 2 The Great Day Notice that Joel 2:31 does not say cosmic disturbances come before the Day of the Lord. It says the cosmic disturbances will not come before the great and awesome Day of the Lord. Is there a difference between "the Day of the Lord" and "the great and awesome day of the Lord?"

Zechariah 14 The Day of the Lord has a broad and narrow sense. Zechariah says, "And **in that Day** His feet will stand on the Mount of Olives, which faces Jerusalem on the east. And the Mount of Olives shall be split in two, from east to west, making a very large valley; half of the mountain shall move toward the north and half of it toward the south. Then you shall flee through My mountain valley, for the mountain valley shall reach to Azal. Yes, you shall flee as you fled from the earthquake in the days of Uzziah, king of Judah. Thus, the LORD my God will come, and all the saints with You. It shall come to pass **in that day** that there will be **no light**; the lights will diminish. It shall be **one day** which is known to the LORD; neither Day nor night. but at evening time it shall happen that it will be light. And **in that day**, it shall be that living waters shall flow from Jerusalem, half of them toward the eastern sea and half of them toward the western sea; in both summer and winter it shall occur. And the LORD shall be King over all the earth. **In that day** it shall be; 'The LORD is one,' and His name one" (Zech. 14:4-9, bold type added).

Zechariah 14 talks about the Day of the Lord (Zech. 14:1). On that Day, the Lord will set foot on the Mount of Olives (Zech. 14:4) and there will be cosmic disturbances (Zech. 4:6-7). The Day of the Lord involves a single day. (see "one day" in verse 8) and it can also refer to a much longer period of time, such as the kingdom (see "the Lord shall be King over all the earth" in verse 9).

Genesis 1 The opening words of the Bible indicate that the word "day" is used in various ways. Genesis says, "And God saw the light that it was good and God divided the light from the darkness. God called the light day and the darkness He called night. So, the evening and the morning were the first day" (Gen. 1:4-5). God called the light Day and the darkness night. Then, He called the evening and the morning day. The word "day" in this passage is used for daylight, that is, the hours between sunrise and sunset and it is used for a 24-hour day. Later in this passage, the word "day" is used for a period longer than 24 hours. Genesis 2:4 says, "This is the history of the heavens and the earth when they were created in the day that the Lord made the earth and the heavens." So, the term "day" in the Bible can mean 1) daylight, 2) 24 hours, 3) A period of time longer than 24 hours. Likewise, the Day of the Lord is used for an extended period and a short period, perhaps 24 hours. We speak of the "day" we were born, meaning a single day and we say, "in my day," meaning a day longer than a single day.

The point is that the expression "the great and awesome day of the Lord" is not a reference to the entire 70th week of Daniel but to a single day. The question is, to what day does it refer? Showers writes, E. W. Bullinger says, "It is called 'the great and the terrible day of the Lord,' as though it were the climax of the whole known as 'the day of the Lord'" (The Apocalypse or The Day of the Lord, p. 248). Along similar lines, C. F. Keil, when referring to the judgment of the narrow Day of Joel 3, declared, 'It is the last decisive judgment, in which all the single judgments find their end' (*The Twelve Minor Prophets*, 1:226)" (Showers, p. 164).

Showers says, "The narrow sense refers to one specific day—the day on which Christ will return to the earth in his glorious Second Coming with his angels" (Showers, p. 162). He cites the Babylonian Talmud, which says the great and terrible Day of the Lord refers "to the advent of the Messiah (Shabbath, 118a, n., p. 580)" (Showers, p. 163). Showers adds, "Because Joel and Malachi were both referring to the same great and terrible Day of the Lord, and because Joel was referring to the narrow day, we can conclude that Malachi's great and terrible day of the Lord is also the narrow day, the day on which Christ will return to the earth in His glorious Second Coming is the grand climax or end of the judgment phase of the broad Day of the Lord" (Showers, p. 165).

Matthew 24 What Jesus says in the Olivet Discourse (Mt. 24-25) proves that the cosmic disturbances are immediately before the Second Coming of Christ, not before the Rapture, as the Pre-Wrath view claims. The proof that Matthew 24:31 refers to the Second Coming is the structure of the Olivet Discourse: 1) Tribulation (Mt. 24:29), 2) His Coming in **glory** (Mt. 24:30-31), 3) parables, etc., (Mt. 24:32- 25:30), 4) a return to speaking about the His Coming in **glory** (Mt. 25:31). The question is, "which coming," the Rapture or the Second Coming?

Notice that Matthew 24:30 speaks of "the Son of Man coming on the clouds of heaven with **power** and great **glory**." Jesus comes in power at the Second Coming, not the Rapture. Even Van Kampen says, "coming 'with power ' refers to judgment." (Van Kampen, p. 301). Furthermore, in Matthew 24:30, the Son of Man comes in His glory. "Glory" ties Matthew 24:30 and Matthew 25:31 together. Matthew 25:31 states, "When the Son of Man comes in His **glory** and all the holy angels with Him, and then He will sit on the **throne** of His glory (Mt. 25:31, bold type added). In other words, this coming is when He establishes the kingdom. So, "When He comes in His glory, then He sits on the throne" (Mt. 25:31) proves that coming in His glory in Matthew 24:30 refers to the Second Coming, not the Rapture. Therefore, the appearance of cosmic disturbances does not support the Pre-Wrath theory; instead, they disprove it because the cosmic disturbances occur before the Second Coming, not the Rapture.

Also, Rosenthal says, "Cosmic disturbance precedes the Day of the Lord" (Rosenthal, p. 152), but Paul taught that the Day of the Lord would come as a thief in the night when people are saying peace and safety (1 Thess. 5:2-3). There is no possibility of any time being "peace and safety" after the second seal because, at the second seal, peace is taken from the earth (Rev. 6:4).

Conclusion: Cosmic disturbances do not come before the Day of the Lord; they appear before the great and awesome Day of the Lord, which is before the Second Coming at the end of the Tribulation.

The Beginning of the Day of the Lord

The Pre-Wrath View The Pre-Wrath view is that the Day of the Lord begins after the Great Tribulation, which means it begins somewhere between the middle and the end of the Tribulation. So, the critical issue is when the Day of the Lord (God's wrath) begins.

The Pre-Wrath view argues that 1) The first four seals of Revelation 6 are not God's wrath; instead, they are man's wrath. 2) The fifth seal marks the beginning of the Great Tribulation in the middle of the 70th week (the Tribulation), but it will not last 3½ years, as it will be shortened. 3) The sixth seal introduces the cosmic disturbances that precede the Day of the Lord. 4) The Rapture is between the sixth and seventh seals. 5) The seventh seal is the beginning of the Day of the Lord (Rosenthal, pp. 137-153, especially the chart on p. 147).

Revelation 6 In the first place, the Day of the Lord, the Day of God's wrath, begins with the first seal (Rev. 6:1-2), not the seventh seal (see the extensive discussion of the seals in the chapter on the Pre-Tribulation Rapture, pp. 9-16). All Revelation 6:17 is saying is that "it is not until the disturbances of the sixth seal, which obviously are caused by God, that the unregenerate recognized that what they have been experiencing with the earlier seals was actually the Day-of-the-Lord wrath" (Showers, p. 79).

Zephaniah 3 Another indication that the Day of the Lord begins before the seventh seal is that, as Rosenthal concedes, the Day of the Lord represents God's judgment of nations (Rosenthal, p. 180). The Day of the Lord is the Day of God's wrath on the entire world (see God's wrath on "all the earth" in Zeph. 3:8). Since the Day of the Lord is God's judgment on the world and the Tribulation begins with God's judgment on the world (Rev. 6:4), the Day of the Lord begins before the seventh seal.

Isaiah 2 Furthermore, the sixth seal does not occur before the Day of the Lord as the Pre-Wrath view claims, but is part of the Day of the Lord. Many commentators point out that the sixth seal is based on Isaiah 2:10-.22. Showers explains, "That prophecy foretold the time and people, including the proud and lofty, will flee to hide in the holes of the rocks and caves of the earth 'with the fear of the Lord and for the glory of his majesty, when he arises to shake terribly the earth' (v. 19). Isaiah describes what John saw in conjunction with Christ breaking the six seal of Revelation 6:12-17. Thus, Isaiah was foretelling the sixth seal. Isaiah indicated that he was writing about the Day of the Lord (v. 12), and that 'in that day' people will 'go into the clefts of the rocks, and into the top of the ragged rock, for fear of the Lord, and for the glory of his majesty' (vv, 20-21). Thus, the language of Isaiah's prophecy signifies that the sixth seal will be within (not before) the Day of the Lord, and, therefore, will involve the day of the Lord's wrath of God" (Showers, p. 77).

Revelation 6:17 The Pre-Wrath view argues that Revelation 6:17 is not part of the Day of the Lord because Joel 2:30-31 states that cosmic disturbances are before the Day of the Lord. Joel 2:30-31 does not say cosmic disturbances come before the Day of the Lord. Read Joel 2:31 carefully. It says, "before the coming of the great and awesome Day of the Lord" (Joel 2:31, bold print added). Revelation 6:17 is not talking about the Day of the Lord; it is talking about "the great day."

Conclusion: The Day of the Lord begins before the Great Tribulation, not after it.

Summary: The Pre-Wrath interpretation of the Rapture that is based on the shortening of the Great Tribulation to less than 3½ years and the beginning of the Day of the Lord's wrath after the shortening of the Great Tribulation is not biblical.

Simply put, the Pre-Wrath position begins by dividing the 70th week of Daniel (commonly called the Tribulation) into three parts: 1) the first half of the 70th week, 2) the Great Tribulation, which is shortened (Mt. 24:22), and 3) the Day of the Lord. Then they reasoned that since the cosmic disturbances are before the Day of the Lord (Joel 2:30-31), the Rapture must take place before the Day of the Lord, which is somewhere between the middle of the 70th week and the end of the 70th week of Daniel. According to their view, the Rapture is, therefore, between the 6th and 7th seal in Revelation 6. Thus, the Pre-Wrath position depends on their interpretation of two verses: Matthew 24:22 and Joel 2:30-31. Since their interpretation of those two verses is wrong, their position is not biblical.

CHAPTER 5

POST-TRIBULATION RAPTURE

The Post-Tribulation Rapture view is that the church will pass through the Tribulation at the end of which the Rapture will occur, but there are variations. Walvoord summarizes the various views of the Post-Tribulation view proposed in recent years (Walvoord, "Post-Tribulationism Today: Part I, pp. 16-25). Alexander Reese (*The Approaching Advent of Christ*, 1937) uses technical terms to refer to "appearing," "the day," "the end," and "revelation" and relates the Rapture to the Second Coming. He also claims that the resurrection of the church occurs at the same time as the resurrection of Revelation 20. J. Barton Payne (*The Imminent Appearing of Christ*, 1962) identifies the Tribulation with the contemporary problems of Christianity. Few have followed Payne. George Ladd (*The Blessed Hope*, 1956) considers the Great Tribulation still future. Christ's return cannot be any day; it will only follow the years required to fulfill prophecies relating to the Tribulation. Robert H. Gundry (*The Church and the Tribulation*, 1973) has developed new arguments for the Post-tribulation Rapture. Gundry's assessment is that Reese's book "has long been out of date, not to mention its embarrassingly bombastic style" and Ladd's book "gained neither the volume of the press nor the exegetical backing which were given to pre-tribulationism" (Gundry, p. 9).

Church History It is often argued that the church has historically held the Post-tribulation position and that the Pre-tribulation view is a new doctrine, beginning with J. N. Derby about 1830 (for example, see Gundry, pp. 172, 188). In the first place, Scripture determines doctrine, not tradition. Be that as it may, as Walvoord points out, "The early church believed in a coming time of trouble, in the imminent coming of the Lord, and in the millennium to follow" (Walvoord, p. 137). He concludes that while the early church did not teach twentieth-century Pre-tribulation, nor did it clearly teach modern Post-tribulation, adding, "It is, therefore, a problem which must be settled based on exegesis of the Scripture rather than by polling the early fathers" (Walvoord, p. 139).

Arguments against Pre-Tribulation Rapture

Deliverance from Wrath Gundry argues that the Greek particle that connects 1 Thessalonians 4 and 5, which he says is δε, does not prove "the beginning of a new thought" (Gundry, p. 105). Therefore, "the Parousia/rapture will mark the beginning of the Day of the Lord, ... the rapture will follow the tribulation" (Gundry, p. 106).

Gundry has misrepresented the Greek text and, therefore, has misinterpreted the passage. In the Greek text, 1 Thessalonians 5:1 begins with περι δε (not just δε) and, as was explained under the discussion of the Pre-tribulation Rapture, Paul uses that construction elsewhere to denote a new and contrasting subject. The new subject is the *time* of the Rapture. The passage teaches that since believers are delivered from the Day of the Lord's wrath and the Day of the Lord's wrath is at the beginning of the Tribulation, the Rapture occurs *before* the Tribulation (for details, see the chapter on the Pre-tribulation Rapture).

Removal of the Restrainer Gundry agrees with Pre-tribulationists that the restrainer is the Holy Spirit (Gundry, pp. 125-128), but he interprets "until he is taken out of the way" to mean "become out of the middle" and says it "does not demand removal from the world" (Gundry, p. 127). In other words, "The restrainer is standing in the middle, i.e., between the *person* of the Antichrist and the *revelation* of the Antichrist," and he must "become out of the middle" (Gundry, p. 127, italics his).

A. T. Robertson renders "taken out of the way" as "removed." *Baker's New Testament Commentary*, which takes the restrainer to be law and order, says, "in spite of objections that have been advanced," 'taken out of the way" is probably a good English equivalent of the Greek idiom" (see "taken out of the way" in the NASB, NIV, and the ESV).

Paul uses this expression in 1 Corinthians 5:2 of a sexually immoral man he wants "taken away" from them by physical death (by "the destruction of the flesh," 1 Cor. 5:5), which would undoubtedly be removal from this world. If 2 Thessalonians 2 is talking about the Holy Spirit and His removal from the world, the Pre-tribulation Rapture explanation makes the most sense because it explains how the Holy Spirit can be taken out of the world dong His work of baptizing people into the body of Christ, but not in His work of regeneration (see the discussion of this passage in the chapter on the Pre-tribulation Rapture).

From the Hour Gundry claims that in dangerous situations, the Greek word translated "keep" in "I will keep you from the hour of trial which shall come upon the whole world" (Rev. 3:10), means "guard" (Gundy, p. 58). He assumes that the church is in the Tribulation and, therefore, needs guarding, but if the point is that the church is being kept from the Tribulation, "keep" is the appropriate translation. The Greek word translated "keep" may mean "guard" in some other places, but translations render it "keep" in Revelation 3:10 (KJV; NKJV; RV; RSV; ASV; NASB; NIV; ESV; ISV; LEB; LITV; MKJV; GNB; Williams; Douay; Young's literal translation).

Gundry also argues that the preposition "from" (ek) means "out from within" (Gundry, p. 55). In other words, the church will be protected in the Tribulation, but the combination "keep from" is used in only one other place in the New Testament, where Jesus says, "I do not pray that you should take them out of the world, but that you should keep them from the evil one" (Jn. 17:15). He is praying for complete deliverance from the evil one not a protection in the evil one. Thus, the promise is to be from the hour of the trial, that is, the period of time. Furthermore, it is simply not true that the Tribulation saints will be protected. They will be persecuted and martyred (Rev. 6:9-19; 7:9, 13, 14; 13:15; 14:13; 16:6; 18:24; 24:4).

Revelation 3:10 was explained in the chapter on the Pre-tribulation Rapture, but here is what Ryrie said in his review of Gundry's book.

"The conclusion [of Gundry] is that the phrase τηρήσω ἐκ τῆς ὥρας means emergence from within the hour or protection issuing in emission. Simply stated, this means that the church will go through the tribulation and emerge from it at its close at the second coming but will be kept in the meantime from the testing of that time. This conclusion is arrived at by examining other possible meanings of ἐκ and choosing 'out from within' as the correct one here by stating that τηρέω means 'guard' and that, thus, the phrase means protection issuing in emission. Again, the temptation to dismember a phrase has caught the author in an exegetical fault. For those for whom the almost tedious discussion of various shades of meaning of these and related words is unhelpful, if not meaningless, they should simply look up τηρέω ἐκ in the lexicon where the specific use in Revelation 3:10 is said to mean 'protect someone from someone or something.' The 'something' from which believers are promised protection is the 'hour' of worldwide trial, which is coming. Apparently, recognizing the force of the total phrase ('kept from the hour'), the author [Gundry] suggests two ways to 'undercut the stress on the term hour' (p. 59). One is to make the usual distinction between the events of the tribulation years and the time itself. The believer, we are told, will be present during the time but will be delivered from the experiences of that time, and in this way, he is kept from the hour. The other suggestion is that the hour of testing is not the entire seventieth week of Daniel (which the author considers to be yet future) but only the very last crisis at the close of the tribulation. This is consistent with his view of the Day of the Lord, but no outline of the sequence of judgments of the Revelation can confine the 'hour of testing which shall come upon the whole earth' to the 'last crisis.' It does not seem that pretribulational exegesis is the one guilty of non sequitur" (Ryrie, Review, pp. 176-177).

For a detailed discussion of Revelation 3:10, see "The Rapture in Revelation 3:10" by Jeffrey Townsend at https://www.pre-trib.org/articles/dr-thomas-ice/message/the-rapture-in-revelation-3-10/read.

The Church in the Tribulation In Revelation, the church is mentioned as being on earth before (chapters 1-3) and after (Rev. 22:16) the Tribulation, but it is not mentioned on earth during the Tribulation. Instead, the church is represented in heaven as twenty-four elders during the Tribulation. Gundry says, "Possibly the twenty-four elders stand for the church. But then, 'elders' may merely denote twenty-four brings, human or celestial, who, quite apart from representation of the whole church as present, have official responsibility for leading the heavenly worship of God, a function we know they perform (4:9-11; 5:8-12)" (Gundry, p. 70).

The identity of the twenty-four elders as a representation of the church in heaven during the Tribulation is determined by what the text says about them. The twenty-four elders are clothed in white (Rev. 4:4), and the church at Sardis was told the overcomers would be clothed in white garments (Rev. 3:5). The twenty-four elders wear crowns of gold (Rev. 4:4), and members of the church are told they will receive crowns (Rev. 2:10; 3:11). Neither angels nor Israel are ever said to wear white robes and gold crowns.

Denial of Imminence Post-tribulationists dismiss the doctrine of imminence by saying that the announcement of events such as the death of Peter (Jn. 21:18-19), the detention of Paul (Acts 23:11), and the destruction of Jerusalem (Lk. 21:20-24) make imminence impossible. Despite those apparent difficulties, many commentators who were not Pre-tribulationist have concluded that the New Testament teaches imminence (see the discussion of imminence in the chapter on Pre-Tribulation Rapture). If believers in the first century could preach and believe in the any-moment Rapture, certainly all believers who lived after the first century could also.

Post-tribulationists who reject the doctrine of imminence say that the passages in the New Testament that Pre-tribulationists use to support the doctrine of imminence teach nothing more than expectance (Gundry, p. 30). Those passages are not just saying expect; they say be ready, implying imminence (*cf.* Mt. 24:42 with Mt. 24:44).

Conclusion: The arguments that the Post tribulationists used to disprove Pre-tribulationism are not biblically sound. Therefore, Post-tribulationists have not disproven Pre-tribulationism.

Arguments for Post-Tribulation Rapture

Through the Tribulation It is also argued that the New Testament teaches that the church will go through tribulations. Paul said, "We must through many tribulations enter the kingdom of God" (Acts 14:22). Granted, the New Testament teaches that believers experience tribulations (plural) in this life, but it also speaks about a Tribulation, during which the wrath of God is poured out on the earth. As has been pointed out, believers will be delivered from the wrath to come, which means they will not go through the Tribulation.

To avoid the conclusion that believers experience the wrath of God, some Post-tribulationists say that the church will experience the wrath of Satan (Gundy, p. 49) or men (Ockenga; see Walvoord, p. 141), but not God. It is like the children of Israel going through the plagues of Egypt but not experiencing them. While the plagues on Egypt were of such a nature that they may have fallen on the Egyptians and not the children of Israel, the judgments of the Tribulation will not be like that. The judgments of the Tribulation include earthquakes, war, and pestilence, which by their very nature are not "suitable for discriminatory judgment" (Walvoord, p. 142). Believers are promised that they will be delivered from the *day* of wrath, that is, the time during which wrath will be poured out upon the earth (Rev. 3:10; Walvoord, p. 142).

The Last Trump Like Mid-tribulationists, the Post-tribulationists use the reference to the last trumpet in 1 Corinthians 15:52 to support their position. The difference between the Mid-tribulationists and the Post-tribulationists is that the Post-tribulationists claim that the last trumpet is at the end of the Tribulation instead of the middle of the Tribulation. The seventh trumpet is at the end of the Tribulation (Reese, p. 73). Identifying the last trumpet of 1 Corinthians 15 with the seventh trumpet of Revelation has been answered (see the chapter on the Mid-tribulation Rapture).

Post-Tribulation Rapture

The Resurrection Citing passages from the Old Testament and the New Testament, Post-tribulationists point out that the Scripture teaches that the resurrection is at the end of the Tribulation just before the kingdom, and, therefore, the Rapture is at the end of the Tribulation. For example, from the Old Testament, both Reeves and Gundry cite Isaiah 25:8, 26:19, and Daniel 12:1-3, 13.

Daniel 12 teaches that *after the Tribulation* (Dan. 12:1), the Old Testament saints will be raised from the dead (Dan. 12:2). Paul taught that *at the Rapture*, "the dead *in Christ* will rise" (1 Thess. 4:16, italics added). In light of these facts, there are two possibilities: 1) There is one resurrection at the end of the Tribulation, which means that the Rapture is at the end of the Tribulation. 2) There are two resurrections, one at the beginning of the Tribulation and the other at the end. Since the Old Testament saints are never described by the phrase "in Christ," the expression "the dead in Christ will rise" (1 Thess. 4:16) includes only the church (Walvoord, p. 154). Therefore, the resurrection at the end of the Tribulation does not prove a Post-tribulation Rapture for the church.

Both Reeves and Gundry cite Luke 14:14-15, Luke 20:3436, and John 6:39, 40, 44, 54; 11:24, where Jesus spoke of the resurrection on the last day, which they interpreted to mean at the end of the Tribulation. Pentecost responds, "All apply to God's program for Israel. If it be shown that this resurrection takes place at the second advent, it does not prove posttribulation rapturism, unless the church must be resurrected at the same time" (Pentecost, p. 200).

Reese says 1 Corinthians 15:50-54 "will settle the whole controversy" because it refers to Isaiah 28:5, which means Paul synchronizes the resurrection with the inauguration of the theocratic Kingdom (Reese, pp. 43-44). Pentecost points out that "Reese's error is in supposing all the righteous dead must be raised at the same time. (Pentecost, p. 201).

Revelation 20:4-6 says, "And I saw thrones, and they sat on them, and judgment was committed to them. Then I saw the souls of those who had been beheaded for their witness to Jesus and for the word of God, who had not worshiped the beast or his image, and had not received his mark on their foreheads or on their hands. And they lived and reigned with Christ for a thousand years. But the rest of the dead did not live again until the thousand years were finished. This is the first resurrection. Blessed and holy is he who has part in the first resurrection. Over such the second death has no power, but they shall be priests of God and of Christ, and shall reign with Him a thousand years" (20:4-6). Ladd says that this is the only explicit statement of Post-tribulationism in the Bible and goes so far as to say that, except for this one passage, he will grant that the Scripture nowhere explicitly states that the church will go through the Great Tribulation (Ladd, p. 165).

So, what does this passage say? 1). John saw that judgment was committed to those sitting on the throne (Rev. 20:4a). This is a reference to the twenty-four elders who represent the church (Walvoord). Christ told the Apostles that they would sit on thrones judging the twelve tribes of Israel (Mt. 19:28; Lk. 22:29). Paul said that the saints would judge the world and angels (1 Cor. 6:2-3). 2)

John saw martyred Tribulation saints who were resurrected will be raised to reign (Revelation 20:4b). The expression "they lived" implies that they were resurrected. 3). The rest of the dead, that is, the wicked dead (Smith), will be raised after the Millennium (Rev. 20:6, 12).

What is the first resurrection? It cannot be in a temporal sequence first since God has already resurrected Jesus Christ (Constable). Christ's resurrection was the first fruit (1 Cor. 15:20). At the time of Christ's resurrection, a "token number" of Old Testament saints were raised (Mt. 27:52-53) as part of the first fruits (Walvoord). Church saints will be raised at the Rapture (1 Thess. 4:16), which is before the Tribulation. The Old Testament saints will be raised at the end of the Tribulation (Dan. 12:1). Therefore, the "first resurrection" is not an event but an "order of resurrection including all the righteous who are raised from the dead before the millennial kingdom begins." They are "first" compared to the wicked dead, who will be raised after the millennium (Walvoord; Smith). As Constable points out, "Other names for this "first" resurrection are the resurrection of the just (Luke 14:14; Acts 24:15), the resurrection from among the dead (Luke 20:34–36), the resurrection of life (John 5:29), and the resurrection to everlasting life (Dan. 12:2)."

Matthew 24:29-31 Jesus said, "Immediately after the tribulation of those days the sun will be darkened, and the moon will not give its light; the stars will fall from heaven, and the powers of the heavens will be shaken. Then the sign of the Son of Man will appear in heaven, and then all the tribes of the earth will mourn, and they will see the **Son of Man** coming on the **clouds** of heaven with power and great glory. And He will send His **angels** with a great sound of a **trumpet**, and they will gather together His **elect** from the four winds, from one end of heaven to the other."

Paul wrote, "For this we say to you by the word of the Lord, that we who are alive and remain until the coming of the Lord will by no means precede those who are asleep. For the **Lord** Himself will descend from heaven with a shout, with the voice of an **archangel**, and with the **trumpet** of God. And the dead in Christ will rise first. Then **we who are alive** and remain shall be caught up together with them in the **clouds** to meet the Lord in the air. And thus we shall always be with the Lord" (1 Thess. 4:15-17).

The Post-tribulation argument is that since both passages speak of the same things: 1) Jesus, 2) believers, 3) angels, 4) trumpets, and 5) clouds, they are both describing the same event. Matthew 24 says this event is the Second Coming of Christ immediately after the Tribulation (Mt. 24:29-30), and 1 Thessalonians 4 describes the Rapture. Therefore, the Rapture is after the Tribulation since these events are the same.

Granted, there are some similarities between Matthew 24 and 1 Thessalonians 4, but there are also differences. Similarities do not prove sameness. Differences demonstrate that similarities are not conclusive proof of sameness. The differences indicate that two different events are being described.

In Matthew, the Son of Man *comes on* the clouds; in 1 Thessalonians, believers are *in them*. In Matthew, the *angels* gather the elect; in 1 Thessalonians, the archangel, who is not mentioned in Matthew 24, speaks (see the voice of the archangel); he does not do anything. In Matthew, *nothing* is said about a resurrection; in 1 Thessalonians, the resurrection is the *central point*. In Matthew, the elect (Jews; see the next paragraph) are gathered *after* Christ's arrival to earth; in 1 Thessalonians, believers are gathered *in the air* (the implication in Jn. 14:1-3 is that they are then taken to heaven). This last comparison alone is sufficient to demonstrate that two entirely different events are being described.

Matthew 24 mentions the elect; 1 Thessalonians 4 does not. Who are the elect in Matthew 24:31? In Isaiah 65:7-16, there is a sharp contrast between the believing Jewish remnant and the unbelieving Israelites. God calls the believing remnant "mine elect" (Isa. 65:9). In the future, the elect remnant of Jews will be greatly blessed on the earth (Isa. 65:17-25; see also Isa. 11:5, 6, 12; Micah 2:12; Ezek. 36:24; 27:21). In Matthew 24, Jesus is speaking about the Jews, which is evident by His references to such things as the holy place (Mt. 24:15), the Sabbath (Mt. 24:20), and the Messiah (Mt 24:23-24) during the Tribulation (Mt. 24:29). In that context, Jesus uses the word "elect" three times (Mt. 24:22, 24, 31). In other words, the elect in Matthew 24:31 refers to believing Jews during the Tribulation.

Matthew 24 says angels will "gather together His elect from the four winds, from one end of heaven to the other." Jesus is using the language of Deuteronomy 30:4-5, which says, "If any of you are driven out to the farthest parts under heaven, from there the Lord will gather you and from there He will bring you. And the Lord your God will bring you to the land which your fathers possessed and you shall possess it." In other words, Jesus is talking about the regathering of Israel after His Second Coming.

Arnold Fruchtenbaum says, "The Matthew passage is a rather simple summary of all that the prophets had to say about the second facet of Israel's final restoration. Its purpose was to make clear that the worldwide regathering predicted by the prophets will be fulfilled only after the second coming" (Fruchtenbaum, cited by Ice).

Showers points out how this is a description of the regathering of Israel rather than the Rapture. "First, because of Israel's persistent rebellion against God, He declared that He would scatter the Jews 'into all the winds' (Ezek. 5:10, 12) or 'toward all winds' (Ezek. 17:21). In Zechariah 2:6, God stated that He did scatter them abroad 'as four winds of the heavens.' ... God did scatter the Jews all over the world. Next, God also declared that in the future, Israel would be gathered from the east, west, north, and south, 'from the ends of the earth' (Isa. 43:5-7). We should note that in the context of this promise, God called Israel His 'chosen' (vv. 10, 20).... Just as Jesus indicated that the gathering of His elect from the four directions of the world will take place in conjunction with 'a great trumpet' (literal translation of the Greek text of Mt. 24:21), so Isaiah 27:13 teaches that the scattered children of Israel will be gathered to their homeland in conjunction with the blowing of 'a great trumpet' (literal translation of the Hebrew). Gerhard Friedrich wrote that in that future eschatological day, 'a great horn shall be blown (Is. 27:13)' and the exiled will be brought back by that signal. Again, he asserted that in conjunction with the blowing of the great trumpet of Isaiah 27:13, 'There follows the gathering of Israel and the return of the dispersed to Zion.' It is significant to note that Isaiah 27:13, which foretells this future regathering of Israel, is the only specific reference in the Old Testament to a 'great' trumpet. Although Isaiah 11:11-12 does not refer to a great trumpet, it is parallel to Isaiah 27:13 because it refers to the same regathering of Israel. In its context, this passage indicates that when the Messiah (a root of Jesse, vv. 1, 10) comes to rule and transform the world as an 'ensign' (a banner), He will gather together the scattered remnant of His people Israel 'from the four corners of the earth' (Showers, cited by Ice).

To sum up, Matthew 24:31 refers to the regathering of Israel after the Second Coming of Christ and 1 Thessalonians 4 describes the Rapture of the church. According to Matthew 24:31, angels will *gather* the elect (Israel) together. According to 1 Thessalonians, the Rapture is the simultaneous resurrection of the dead saints and the *catching up* of living saints together with them in the clouds to meet the Lord in the air (1 Thess. 4:15-17). Jesus will receive them *to Himself* (Jn. 14:3).

The cleansing of the Temple illustrates that similarity does not determine sameness. John says, "After this, He went down to Capernaum, He, His mother, His brothers, and His disciples; and they did not stay there many days. Now, the Passover of the Jews was at hand, and **Jesus** went up to Jerusalem. And He found in the **temple** those who **sold oxen and sheep and doves**, and the money changers doing business. When He had made a whip of cords, He drove them all out of the temple, with the sheep and the oxen, and poured out the changers' money and **overturned the tables**. And **He said** to those who sold doves, "Take these things away! Do not make My Father's house a house of merchandise!" (Jn. 2:12-16).

Matthew states, "Then **Jesus** went into the **temple** of God and drove out all those who bought and sold in the temple, and **overturned the tables** of the money changers and the seats of those who **sold doves**. And **He said** to them, "It is written, 'MY HOUSE SHALL BE CALLED A HOUSE OF PRAYER,' but you have made it a 'DEN OF THIEVES'" (Mt. 21:12-13).

Mark puts it this way, "So they came to Jerusalem. Then **Jesus** went into the **temple** and began to drive out those who bought and sold in the temple and **overturned the tables** of the money changers and the seats of those who **sold doves.** And He would not allow anyone to carry wares through the temple. Then He taught, **saying** to them, 'Is it not written, 'MY HOUSE SHALL BE CALLED A HOUSE OF PRAYER FOR ALL NATIONS'? But you have made it a 'DEN OF THIEVES'" (Mk. 11:15-17).

Luke records, "Then **He** went into the **temple** and began to drive out those who bought and **sold** in it, **saying** to them, 'It is written, 'MY HOUSE IS A HOUSE OF PRAYER,' but you have made it a 'DEN OF THIEVES'" (Lk. 19:45-46).

Since the Gospel of John and the synoptic Gospels speak of the same things: 1) Jesus, 2) Temple, 3) selling doves, 4) overturning the tables, and 5) Jesus speaking, they are describing the same event. Therefore, since the two accounts describe the same event, Jesus only cleansed the Temple once.

Granted, there are some similarities between the Gospel of John and the synoptic Gospel's account of the cleansing of the Temple, but there are also differences. John clearly places the cleansing of the Temple *at the beginning* of Jesus' ministry. He says the first miracle was turning water into wine at Cana and "after this," Jesus went to Capernaum, where He stayed "a few days." Then he says that since the Passover was at hand, Jesus went to Jerusalem, where He cleansed the Temple (John 2:11-16). The synoptic Gospels place the cleansing of the Temple in the week before the crucifixion.

Aside from their being nearly three years apart, there are differences between the two events. In the first cleansing, Temple officials confronted Jesus immediately (Jn. 2:18), whereas in the second cleansing, the chief priests and scribes confronted Him the following day (Mt. 21:23-27). In the first event, Jesus made a whip of cords to drive out the sellers, but there is no mention of a whip in the second cleansing. Therefore, Jesus cleansed the Temple twice.

Similarities do not prove sameness. Differences demonstrate that similarities are not conclusive proof of sameness. The differences indicate that two different events are being described.

The End In the parable of the wheat and the tares, Jesus says, "At the time of the harvest I will say to the reapers, 'First gather together the tares and bind them into bundles to burn them, but gather the wheat into my barns'" (Mt. 13:30). Gundry says that the wheat represents the Rapture, which is a postscript to the law (Gundry, p. 142). The order of events in this parable does not fit either the Pre-tribulation or the Post-tribulation Rapture. The tares are gathered first. As Pentecost observes, "The purpose of Matthew 13 is not to divulge the history of the church, but the history of the kingdom in its mystery form. The time is not that of the church—from Pentecost to the rapture—but the entire age from the rejection of Christ to His coming reception" (Pentecost, p. 202).

Conclusion: The arguments Post-tribulationists use to prove their position are not biblically correct. Therefore, Post-tribulationism is not biblical.

Summary: The Post-tribulation view of the Rapture that assumes that the church will go through the Tribulation (Acts 14:22), that the last trumpet is at the end of the Tribulation, that the resurrection of Daniel 12 includes the church at the end of the Tribulation, that Matthew 24:31 describes the Rapture, and the expression "the end" (Mt. 13:30) is not biblical.

Gundry's book is more of an attack on Pre-tribulationism than an exposition of his view of Post-tribulationism. Ryrie says Gundry's system of Post-tribulationism forces either the exegesis or the system and that it is not easy to explain it because it is

Post-Tribulation Rapture

not systematized (Ryrie, Review, pp. 178-179). Here is Ryrie's summary of "some of the salient features" (Ryrie, Review, p. 179). "The seventieth week of Daniel is yet future, and the church will be on earth during that period (p. 49). The **144,000** will be a group of unsaved people who will be supernaturally protected from dying during that period so that they accept the Lord when He comes at the second coming and be those who populate the millennial kingdom (p. 82). The **twenty-four elders** are twenty-four beings who lead the worship of God in heaven (p. 70). On the earth, the church will not suffer the penal judgments of God but will endure persecution from other quarters (p. 51). She will be looking for the Lord's return, though it will not be imminent, and yet it will be in some sense imminent since the days will be shortened and no one can predict the time of Christ's return (p. 42). The **Day of the Lord** will not begin with the tribulation or any part of it (p. 95), and yet it may begin before Armageddon because there may be a **peaceful lull** at that point (p. 92), which lull will fit somehow into the sequence of seal, trumpet, and bowl judgments which will find somewhat concurrent fulfillment (p. 75). The promise of Revelation 3:10 will be fulfilled when the church emerges from within the tribulation at its end. Then the Lord comes for His saints, meeting them in the air and continuing to descend with them to the earth (p. 159). There will be no formal judgment of living Israel at this point, but only a purging out of the rebels as the Lord brings them toward the promised land through heathen countries (p. 168). The so-called judgment of living Gentiles (**the sheep and the goats**) does not occur at the second coming but after the millennium (p. 166). Believers will not be judged until after the millennium, though they will receive their crowns of rewards at the second coming (Ryrie, Review, p. 169, bold added).

Based on the scenario given by the Lord, the Post-tribulation position is not possible. Jesus said, "When the Son of Man comes in His glory, and all the holy angels with Him, then He will sit on the throne of His glory. All the nations will be gathered before Him, and He will separate them one from another, as a shepherd divides *his* sheep from the goats. And He will set the sheep on His right hand, but the goats on the left. Then the King will say to those on His right hand, "Come, you blessed of My Father, inherit the kingdom prepared for you from the foundation of the world" (Mt. 25:31-34). Post-tribulations teaches that the Rapture takes place at the end of the Tribulation. In other words, according to that view, the saints are caught up to meet the Lord in the air and return from the air together, but the picture painted by the Lord is that He would separate the saints and sinners *after* He returned to the earth. Hence, the Post-tribulation position is impossible because, according to it, the separation of the sheep and the goats occurs *after* the Lord returns to the earth.

Post-tribulationism poses a problem for Post-tribunctionists who are also Pre-millennials, namely, those who will remain in earthly bodies to populate the millennial kingdom. If, as Post-tribulation must say, the Rapture takes place at the end of the Tribulation, then all the saints have glorified bodies; therefore, there would be no one left with an earthly body to enter the millennium.

In addressing this problem, Gundry says, "We are therefore forced to put the judgment of nations after the millennium. For if it were to be placed beforehand, none of the wicked (goats) could enter the millennium" (Gundry, pp. 166-167). In his review of Gundry's book, Ryrie says, "This is strange exegesis for a premillennialist (which Dr. Gundry is), for the Scripture is quite plain as to the time of the judgment as being 'when the Son of man shall come in his glory' and when He shall 'sit upon the throne of his glory' (Matt. 25:31). His understanding of this verse is that there is a gap within it of the thousand years of the millennium so that the judgment of the sheep and goats comes after the millennium.

"But where will believers in earthly bodies come from to populate the millennial kingdom? The author has two suggestions: either the judgment of believers will not take place until the seventy-five days after the second coming (Dan. 12:12) which presumably would allow for some to believe after the posttribulational rapture and then be judged during those seventy-five days and enter the kingdom in earthly bodies (p. 164), or he thinks that the 144,000 will continue as sealed believers during the entire tribulation and then turn to Christ at the second coming and be those who populate the millennial earth (p. 82). Apparently, he does not explain how they can be on earth during all this time and sing 'a new song before the throne, and before the four living ones, and the elders' (Rev. 14:3). In summary, perhaps the clearest thing said about this question is the admission that posttribulationalism is 'forced' into their possible answers" (Ryrie, Review, p. 78).

"In My Father's house are many mansions; if it were not so, I would have told you. I go to prepare a place for you. And if I go and prepare a place for you, I will come again and receive you to Myself; that where I am, there you may be also" (Jn. 14:2-3). The expression "My Father's house" refers to heaven (Barclay; Morris). The Greek word translated "mansions" means "abode, station." It was used of a station on a road where travelers found refreshments. The fact that there will be *many* such places is an indication that there will be room for all. The most natural way to understand "If I go to prepare a place for you, I will *come again*, and receive you to Myself, is not a reference to Pentecost or a believer's death, as some supposed, but a reference to His Second Coming.

These statements indicate that Jesus would return while the apostles were still alive. The passage also seems to imply that since He went to prepare a place for *them*, He would take *them* to that *place*. John Gill (1697-1771), a British Baptist pastor, theologian, and staunch Calvinist who lived more than half a century before Darby, said John 14:2 means, "I will take you up with me to heaven; I will receive you into glory." Alexander Maclaren (1826-1910) wrote Jesus takes "those for whom He had prepared the place to the place which He had prepared for them." This scenario eliminates post-tribulationism, which involves Jesus meeting believers in the air and *returning to the earth*.

Gundry argues that the Greek word translated "mansion" means "abode or an abiding place" and the remainder of the Upper Room Discourse indicates that it is a "spiritual abode in Christ rather than a material structure in heaven" (Gundry, p. 154). He then points to John 14:23, where Jesus said if anyone loves Him and keeps His word, He and the Father would make their abode with them (Gundry, p. 154). That interpretation is nonsense, a word that means "makes no sense." Jesus said He was going to "prepare a *place* for you" (He said that twice), not have an abiding relationship with them!

Post-tribulationists claim the wrath of God is not poured out until the end of the Tribulation. Ryrie points out, "Revelation 15:1 states that the last series of plagues (the bowl judgments) finished, or complete the wrath (literally, anger) of God on the earth. No one debates that the seven bowl judgments must come to pass before God's anger can be finished. The question is not, when will God's anger be finished? The question is, when will it begin? If something is going to be finished when certain events occur, then by all the principles of normal understanding, something must have begun before these events. The seven bowl judgments complete God's wrath; therefore, the wrath of God does not begin with the judgments. It has to begin before. The wrath of God will be finishing, not beginning, at the time of the seven bowl judgments.... Does not Revelation 15:1 negate the claim that God's anger will be limited to the very end of the Tribulation?" (Ryrie, Review, pp. 109-110).

CHAPTER 5
CONCLUSION

So, what is the conclusion? This material has focused solely on the time of the Rapture. It seems to me there is clear and convincing support for the Pre-tribulation Rapture. That is my conclusion, but that's not the bottom line in the Bible. Let me explain.

In 1 Thessalonians 5, after making the point that the day of the Lord begins unexpectedly (1 Thess. 5:1-2), that unbelievers will be suddenly and surely destroyed (1 Thess. 5:3), and that believers will be suddenly and safely delivered (1 Thess. 5:4-5), Paul concludes ("therefore" in 5:6) "Therefore let us not sleep, as others do" (1 Thess. 5:6a). The word "sleep" in 1 Thessalonians 5:6 is different than the one used in 1 Thessalonians 4:13-15. The one used in 1 Thessalonians 5:6 is a figure of speech for moral and spiritual insensibility. Frame says, "It covers all sorts of moral laxity." Hiebert suggests it "denotes indifference to spiritual realities on the part of believers." The phrase "as others do" refers to unbelievers (Alford).

These words seem to focus on Paul's major concern in this passage. Perhaps the Thessalonians were weary under the burden of their trials. They were suffering persecution. The recent death of some of the saints may have suggested to them that expecting the Lord's return in their lifetime was in error. These stresses had become a sedative that was tending to dull their spiritual sensitivity and lull them to sleep.

Paul urges them not to get tired, to relax, and to fall asleep. "But let us watch and be sober" (1 Thess. 5:6b). Being watchful and sober, that is, not drunk, is the opposite of being asleep (Hiebert). The figure of "watching" is used elsewhere in the Scripture of being morally alert, vigilant against the assaults of unrighteousness (Frame). Perhaps, too, there is implied in watching, looking for the return of the Lord (Titus 2:13). Sobriety is also a Scriptural metaphor for moral alertness (Milligan). The spiritually sober man is rational and in control of his senses. He is free from the stupefying effects of sin (Hiebert).

It is almost as if, at this point, Paul says, "Let me illustrate." He says, "For those who sleep, sleep at night, and those who get drunk are drunk at night" (1 Thess. 5:7). The word "for" indicates that this statement is made as an explanation of what was said in verse 6. Alford suggests that this is an explanation of the phrase "as others do" in verse 6. Paul is not using sleep, night, and drunkenness in this in the figurative sense (Lightfoot). Instead, he argues that it is natural and normal for men to sleep at night, and those who get drunk usually do it after dark. While drunkenness was common in the ancient world, it was associated with the night (today, it is associated with the weekend, especially the three-day weekend). To be drunk during the day was unusual and unlikely (Acts 2:15).

Paul's explanation/illustration is that sleep and drunkenness are naturally associated with night, so spiritual slumber and sin are characteristics of spiritual darkness. Believers are not of that realm and, therefore, should not sleep. They should be awake and sober. Thus far in this passage, Paul has spoken in figurative terms. Believers are not of the darkness or of the night, so they should not sleep or get drunk. They are of the light and the day; therefore, they should watch and be sober. Specifically, how is this done?

Paul now explains. He says, "But let us who are of the day be sober, putting on the breastplate of faith and love, and as a helmet the hope of salvation" (1 Thess. 5:8). In the Greek text, "let us" is emphatic and "sober" is in the present tense. Paul insists that spiritual sobriety should be the habit of the believer (Hiebert). Paul has told the Thessalonians that they are of the light of the day, and, therefore, they should not sleep but wake up and watch and not get drunk but be sober. Now, he tells them to get dressed. He exhorts them to put on two pieces of defensive armor, a breastplate and a helmet. Believers are not only watchmen; they are warriors (Hiebert). They must not only be awake and watching but also be equipped to resist the onslaught of the enemy. The breastplate covered the soldier's body from the neck to the waist, protecting his heart, and the helmet covered his head (Hiebert).

Later in his life, Paul used the imagery of a breastplate and a helmet to convey spiritual truth, but when he did, he changed the figure. Here, the breastplate consists of the dual spiritual virtues of faith and love. In Ephesians 6:14, the breastplate consists of righteousness. In this passage, the helmet includes the hope of salvation, whereas in Ephesians 6:17, it is simply salvation. Paul uses the same illustration, namely the breastplate and the helmet, to illustrate different spiritual truths.

Being sober consists of faith and love. Throughout 1 Thessalonians, Paul has been concerned about their faith (1 Thess. 3:5, 6, 7, 10). There is no question but that they genuinely trusted Jesus Christ and that faith had provoked them to service (1 Thess. 1:3, 9). Yet, as is the case with all believers, there was still room for growth (1 Thess. 3:10). Thus, Paul urges them to continue to walk by faith (Gal. 2:20; Rom. 1:17). They were to constantly believe God's Word and trust Him for the power to implement it in their lives. Also, throughout this epistle, Paul has been concerned about their love. He acknowledges that they were practicing love (1 Thess. 1:3; 3:6; 4:9), yet again, as is true with all believers, there was room for growth, so Paul prays and urges them to increase in love (1 Thess. 3:12; 4:10).

Being sober consists of "the hope of salvation." The Greek word translated "hope" means "expectation." Why are believers urged to expect salvation? Are they not already saved? In the sense of being saved from the penalty of sin, which is death, the answer is "Yes," but that is not the kind of salvation Paul is speaking about here. The Greek word translated "salvation" means "deliverance" and, in this context, refers to deliverance from the Day of the Lord, which is the Tribulation. This is another way of saying that they should be "looking for the blessed hope and glorious appearing of our great God and Savior Jesus Christ" (Titus 2:13). The hope here is the blessed hope of the Lord's return for His own and the resultant deliverance from the Tribulation to follow. Paul explains that (see "for" in verse 9) in the next verse.

Conclusion

Summary: Since the Day of the Lord is coming unexpectedly, sinners will be suddenly and surely destroyed, and saints will be suddenly and safely delivered, saints should wake up, be alert, and get dressed to live godly lives of faith, love, and hope.

Believers are not of the darkness or the night. They are of the light and the day. Therefore, Paul urges them not to sleep like sinners of the night but to wake up, get dressed, and look out for the dangers that lurk in a sinful world. They are to be mindful of being awake, of what they wear (spiritually speaking) and of watching. Their attitude, their attire, and their actions are critical. They are not to get drunk but to be sober, which means they are to grow in faith, love, and hope. Having said that, Paul, in a sense, has reached the climax of the epistle.

Some Christians appear to be awake, but they're not. For example, you can be active in church and be spiritually asleep. It's called spiritual sleepwalking! In the animal Kingdom, a horse can doze off while standing up, a huge hippopotamus can snore as it floats in the water, and a bat can nap while hanging by its feet. The issue is not whether you are standing, floating, or walking. The question is, "Are you awake, or are you asleep?"

BIBLIOGRAPHY

Abbott-Smith, G. *A Manuel Greek Lexicon of the New Testament.* Edinburgh: T & T Clark, 1960 (reprint of the 1937 edition).

Alexander, Joseph Addison. *The Gospel According to Matthew.* Lynchburg, VA: James Family Christian Publishers, ND (originally published in 1861).

Alford, Henry. *The Greek New Testament.* Revised by Everett F. Harrison. Chicago: Moody Press, 1958.

Arndt, William and Gingrich, F. Wilbur, translated by Walter Bauer. *A Greek-English Lexicon of the New Testament and Other Early Christian Literature.* Chicago: The University of Chicago Press. 1979.

Barnhouse, Donald Grey. *Thessalians, An Exposition Commentary.* Grand Rapids: Zondervan Publishing House, 1977.

Brainard, Lee W. *Ten Potent Proofs for the Pretribulation Rapture.* Soothkeep Press, 2024.

Brown, Francis, Driver, S. R, Briggs, Charles A. ed. *Hebrew and English Lexicon of the Old Testament.* London: Oxford, 1962.

Chisholm, Robert B., Jr. "Joel." In *The Bible Knowledge Commentary: Old Testament*, Edited by John F. Walvoord and Roy B. Zuck. Wheaton: Scripture Press Publications, Victor Books, 1985.

Constable, Thomas, "Dr. Constable's Expository (Bible Study) Notes." Available at http://www.soniclight.com/constable/notes.htm.

Cooper, David L. *Future Events Revealed*. Los Angeles: Biblical Research Society, 1935.

Creed, John Martin. *The Gospel According to St. Luke*. London: MacMillan & Co., 1965 (reprint of the 1930 edition).

Dana and Mantey, *A Manual Grammar of the Greek New Testament*. New York: Macmillan, 1958.

Frame, James Everett. *A Critical and Exegetical Commentary on the Epistles of St. Paul to the Thessalonians*. International Critical Commentary series. Edinburgh: T. & T. Clark, 1912. Rapids: Baker Book House, 1982.

France, R. T. *Matthew, The Tyndale New Testament Commentaries*. Grand Rapids: William B. Eerdmans Publishing Company, 1985.

Geldenhuys, Normal. *Commentary on Luke*, The New International Commentary Series. Grand Rapids: Eerdmans, 1983.

Gill, John. *John Gill's Exposition of the Bible*. e-sword.net.

Gundry, Robert H. *The Church and the Tribulation*, Grand Rapids: Zondervan Publishing House, 1973.

Harrison, Norman B. *The End. Rethinking the Revelation*. Minneapolis: The Harrison Service, 1941.

Hart, John F. "Should Pretribulationists Reconsider the Rapture In Matthew 24:36–44 Part 3 of 3. Journal of the Grace Evangelical Society, vol. 1, Autumn 2008, Num. 41.

Hendriksen, William and Simon J. Kistemaker. *Baker's New Testament Commentary*. Baker Book House. e-sword.net.

Hodges, *Zane*. "1 Thessalonians 5:1–11 and the Rapture," *Chafer Theological Seminary Journal* 6 (October–December 2000).

Hiebert, D. Edmond. *The Thessalians Epistle*. Chicago: Moody Press, 1971.

Ice, Thomas. "Matthew 24:31: Rapture Or Second Coming?" Modified on Oct. 10, 2016. https://www.raptureready.com/2015/04/10/matthew-2431-rapture-or-second-coming-by-thomas-ice/

Ironside, H. A. *Addresses on the First Epistle to the Corinthians*. New York: Loizeaux Brothers Publishers, 1938.

Keil, Carl Friedrich. *The Twelve Minor Prophets*. 2 vols. Translated by James Martin. Biblical Commentary on the Old Testament. Reprint ed. Grand Rapids: Wm. B. Eerdmans Publishing Co., 1949.

Kurschner, Alan E. *Pre-Wrath a Very Short Introduction*. Pompton. Lakes, NJ, 2014.

Ladd, George E. *Critical Questions about the Kingdom of God.*

_____ *The Blessed Hope*, Grand Rapids: Wm. B. Eerdmans Publishing Co., 1956.

Mason Jr., Clarence E. "The Day of Our Lord Jesus Christ," *Bibliotheca Sacra*, vol. 125, no. 500, Oct.-Dec. 1968, pp. 352-359, esp. p. 359.

McClain, Alva J. *The Greatest of the Kingdom*. Chicago: Moody Press, 1959.

Milligan, George. *St. Paul's Epistles to the Thessalonians*. Evangelical Masterworks series. Reprint ed. Old Tappan, N.J.: Fleming H. Revell, Co., n. d.

Mitton, C. Leslie. *The Epistle of James*. Grand Rapids: Wm. B. Eerdmans Publishing Co., 1966.

Moo, Douglas J. *The Letter of James.* Grand Rapids: Wm. B. Eerdmans Publishing Co., 1985.

Morris, Henry M. *The Genesis Record* Grand Rapids: Baker Book House, 1976.

Morris, Leon. *The Gospel According to John.* The New International Commentary on the New Testament. Grand Rapids: William B. Eerdmans Publishing Company, 1984.

_____. *The Revelation of St. John.* Tyndale New Testament Commentary series. Reprint ed., Leicester, England: Inter-Varsity Press, and Grand Rapids: Wm. B. Eerdmans Publishing Co., 1984.

Mounce, Robert H. *The Book of Revelation.* New International Commentary on the New Testament series. Grand Rapids: William B. Eerdmans Publishing Co., 1983.

McNeile, Alan Hugh. *The Gospel According to Matthew.* London: MacMillan & Co. LTD, 1961 (originally published in 1915)..

Niemelä, John. "For You Have Kept My Word: The Grammar of Revelation 3:10." Chafer Theological Seminary: *Chafer Theological Seminary Journal,* Volume 6. 2000.

NKJV Study Bible. Edited by Earl D. Radmacher. Nashville: Thomas Nelson Publishers, 1997.

Payne, J. Barton. *The Imminent Appearing of Christ*, Grand Rapids: Wm. B. Eerdmans Publishing Co., 1962.

Pentecost, J. Dwight. *The Word and Works of Jesus Christ.* Grand Rapids: Zondervan, 1981.

Pickering, Wilbur N. *The Greek New Testament According to Family 35*, 2015.

Bibliography

Plummer, Alfred. *An Exegetical Commentary of The Gospel According to S. Matthew*. Minneapolis: James Family Christian Publishers, ND.

_____. *The Gospel According to St. Luke*, International Critical Commentary Series. New York: Charles Scribner's Sons, 1903.

_____ *The Gospel According to St. John*. The Cambridge Bible for Schools and Colleges, Cambridge: University Press, 1902.

Pentecost, J. Dwight. *Things to Come*, Findley, Ohio: Dunham Publishing Company, 1958.

Reese, Alexander. *The Approaching Advent of Christ*. London: Morgan & Scott, 1937.

Rosenthal, Marvin. *The Pre-Wrath Rapture of the Church*. Nashville: Thomas Nelson Publishers, 1990.

Ryrie, Charles C. *A Survey of Bible Doctrine*, Chicago: Moody Press, 1972.

_____ *Basic Theology*, Wheaton, Illinois, Victor Books, 1986.

_____ *First and Second Thessalians*. Chicago: Moody Press, 1959.

_____ "The Church and the Tribulation: A Review" *Bibliotheca Sacra*, 131:522, April 1974, pp. 173-179.

_____. *The Ryrie Study Bible*. Chicago: Moody Press, 1978.

Showers, E. Renald. *The Pre-Wrath Rapture View*. Grand Rapids: Kregel Publishers, 2001.

Smith, J. B., *A Revelation of Jesus Christ*. Scottdale, Pa.: Herald, 19 61

Stanton, Gerald B. *Kept from the Hour*. Grand Rapids: Zondervan Publishing House, 1956.

Swete, Henry Barclay. *The Apocalypse of St. John*. London: Macmillan Publishers Ltd, 1906.

Tasker, R. V. G. *Matthew,* The Tyndale New Testament Commentaries. Grand Rapids: William B. Eerdmans Publishing Company, 1961.

Toussaint, Stanley D. "Acts." In *The Bible Knowledge Commentary: New Testament*, pp. 349-432. Edited by John F. Walvoord and Roy B. Zuck. Wheaton: Scripture Press Publications, Victor Books, 1983

_____. *Behold the King*. Portland, OR: Multnomah Press, 1980.

Unger, Merrill F. *Zechariah*. Grand Rapids: Zondervan Publishing House, 1963.

Van Kampen, Robert. *The Rapture Question Answered*. Grand Rapids: Fleming H. Revell, 1997.

Walvoord, John F. *Matthew: Thy Kingdom Come*. Chicago: Moody Press, 1974.

_____ "Posttribulationism Today: Part I, The Rise of Posttribulational Interpretation" *Bibliotheca Sacra*, 132:525, January 1975.

_____ *The Blessed Hope and the Tribulation*. Grand Rapids: Zondervan, 1976.

_____ *The Rapture Question*, Rapids: Zondervan Publishing House, 1973.

_____ *The Revelation of Jesus Christ*. Chicago, IL: Moody Press, 1966.

About The Author

G. Michael Cocoris is a gifted communicator. He can make even complicated subjects simple, clear, and practical. His breadth of experience has allowed him to relate to a wide range of audiences.

Michael received a Bachelor of Arts degree from Tennessee Temple University, a Master of Theology degree from Dallas Seminary, and a Doctorate of Divinity from Biola University. He traveled the United States for over a dozen years as a speaker. He has also been a seminary professor, visiting lecturer, and world traveler, including hosting tours to Israel and China.

Michael has pastored three churches, including a rural church when he was in seminary, an urban church, the historic Church of the Open Door, first in downtown Los Angeles and later in Glendora, California, and a suburban church, the Lindley Church in Tarzana California, a suburb of Los Angeles. While at the Church of Open Door, he had a daily radio broadcast.

Michael has written numerous magazine articles, mainly for *Biblical Research Monthly*. He has authored a number of books, including *Seventy Years on Hope Street, A History of the Church of the Open Door*; *How To Live A Biblical Spiritual Life, Clarifying the Confusion; Repentance, The Most Misunderstood Word in the Bible; Evangelism: A Biblical Approach; The Salvation Controversy; Lordship Salvation: Is It Biblical?; The Books of the Bible, the Subject, Structure, Situation, and Significant Verses of Each Book; Psalms, A Song for Every Situation, Each Summarized on One Page;* and *Counseling Theories, A Biblical Evaluation.* In addition, he was a contributor to The *NKJV Study Bible* and *Nelson's New Illustrated Bible Commentary.*

Michael is the pastor of the Lindley Church in Tarzana, California. He and his wife, Patricia, live in Santa Monica, California.

www.ingramcontent.com/pod-product-compliance
Lightning Source LLC
Chambersburg PA
CBHW070119080526
44586CB00013B/1335